THE WORDS, I HOPE, ARE PEARLS FOR LAURE.
THE BOOK, ITSELF, IS FOR THE NAMES WITHIN.

Love
Madness
fishing

Dexter Petley.

LITTLE TOLLER BOOKS

Published by Little Toller Books in 2016
Lower Dairy, Toller Fratrum, Dorset

Text © Dexter Petley 2016

The right of Dexter Petley to be identified as the author of this work has been asserted by him in accordance with Copyright, Design and Patents Act 1988

Jacket and chapter illustrations © Michael Kirkman 2016

Typeset in Garamond by Little Toller Books

Printed by TJ International Ltd, Padstow, Cornwall

All papers used by Little Toller Books are natural, recyclable products made from wood grown in sustainable, well-managed forests

A catalogue record for this book is available from the British Library

All rights reserved

ISBN 978-1-908213-44-0

PREFACE

THIS IS NOT A BOOK for anglers only. What began as a collection of observations on people and places has become a book about childhood and growing up. My intention to write of post-war changes in rural life and nature turned easily and naturally into memorials to the dead. But whatever kind of book it is, angling memoir or a roll call of village tragedy, these are stories which begin and end at the water's edge, written with that particular scrutiny of a fisherman, often the only human being out there to witness either the joys or the sufferings of others.

If you are not an angler, you probably don't realise how close you were to becoming one. Perhaps as close as the leaf you failed to catch in a gust of wind; the sniper who called it a day as you wandered by; the book you never got for Christmas, or the minnow which ignored your worm when you were six. You might feel my observations passing through what you already know, or have seen with your own eyes; or they might touch the empty corner you once reserved for what might have been, in another life.

To be an angler is to accept the rigours of the dreamer in dystopia. The end is disillusion, the beginning is worth it. There is only one beginning to an angler's life, one version of the coming of the rod. It's imprinted in the feel of every cork handle ever after, the smell of every roach in the world or the sound of every downpour on a farm pond. It's enough to carry you most of the way.

If that beginning does come right, it's a fluke cast, beginner's luck; the hook snags your heart and you're an angler in childhood. If you're wise, you stay an angler for life, all the way to the marble keep net or the dead bait can. The pity of it is, you cannot deliberately pass angling on like you might a good book, or an heirloom. You cannot make the child a certain gift of it. There's a fatal responsibility in taking a child fishing for the first time. As a state of being, it's always accidental. There's a mystical fork in the path to the river. You can lead anyone to water, but you can't make them fish.

One Sunday in 2001, I carried my own childhood memories like that heirloom into the early March sunshine. Laure's young 'uns had insisted I pack my fishing rod with the picnic hamper, the bicycles, football and kite, before we set off for *Lac des Settons,* up in the mountains of the Morvan in Burgundy. Tobias was seven, Aloyse five. I played it lightly, deciding I would simply cast a float nearby, like it was a yacht on a string or any other game. They could join in, watch, tangle in the tree, whatever fishing suggested. Catching a fish was not an objective.

It could have been perilous, taking over from their father who lost custody through his own sense of infallibility. He took them fishing once to show us all what a great fisherman he was. Naturally, we lost interest. It wasn't funny, his garden cane rod with terry clips and gaffer tape, his shipping knots and ball-bearing sinkers, his boasting in the face of mishap.

But on the picnic, the children threw logs in every time I cast, and it was fun. No *watch me,* no shooshing, or *sit still you'll scare the fish* nonsense. That comes later, if the gaze is true. The water was cold and clear and nothing stirred in the icy crosswind. In the evening we saw a great mob of roach spawning in the shallows. I found a dead perch with green fur on one flank, like an old rabbit. I put it on the hook when they weren't looking and made a great game of playing a stiff in the margins. We all had a go. The evening sun set on a calm lake dimpled with fry. Aloyse held the rod like a Victorian missionary posing with a shrunken head. Tobias bumped his fingers over the red silk whippings in some ritual of secret whispering. Before bedtime they had both drawn pictures of me and the rod from memory. Its mystery transmitted, they drew the intermediate whippings like measures on a ruler, the reel handle in exactly the right place and even the float had a red tip and was attached bottom end only; more than I remembered, more than I'd hoped to accomplish on a Sunday afternoon. Thirteen years later, there's no sign that either of them will set foot near water, or ever touch a fishing rod again.

Games of chance risk foul-hooking somebody's life, taking as much away as they bestow. A person might never know happiness unless they are fishing; or they might never attain contentment because they never fished. Angling is one of those pastimes you rarely discover for yourself. It's remarkable how often anglers are asked to take other people's children fishing, like it's a rite of passage, but one not quite understood; *I don't know where it's come from*, these bemused parents often say. Perhaps some things are best left to other kids. The imposition of the rod is taboo. You can spook the child into the depths of other dead-ends.

As if to remind me, news comes in as I write of a boy I taught to fish ten years ago. Two days I have never forgotten, carefree days on the edge of the tragic, like it was the summer of 1939, or a day in a Virginia Woolf novel. Two Bloomsbury families in their summer house on the Brittany Coast, the Range Rovers and hats and old poetry books on oak shelves. Confined to indoors by rain, fishing was 'got up' like a trip to the lighthouse for the next bright day. I remember the excitement and expectation, the tumble of questions on the drive to Super U, the present dull world a blur through wipers on full speed. We were shameless, buying the rod and reel off the shelf, the life-like shads in bubble packs, the silver lures which everyone admired. We seemed set up for a better life.

Then the wait, the rain battering the window, the throaty laughter of the public school dads who worked in the city and at the BBC, the charades and popping corks, the women reading novels and singing French songs as they sighed at the window. In the watery sun between downpours, I took the boy casting off rocks in the harbour. Life suddenly made sense to him. He seemed to get it, the certainty that he would become a fisherman and shake off the weight, the choirboy treadmill of the path to Oxford, the sensitive hysterics of a gifted child with haunted eyes. I must admit I drove home feeling uncomfortable with the encounter, that the boy had only stepped outside himself and become more vulnerable because fishing was another thing he was expected to excel at. I don't believe young Harry did become a fisherman. Instead, he became what his parents had created for him. I never saw him again, but I've just been told that he's hanged himself, aged twenty-one.

I wouldn't dare suggest that fishing could have been, for him, a thing to live for, or that fishing soothes any troubled mind. Angling is as much a path to misery as anything else. It can put you at peace with the world, or at odds with it. This is what makes it fit for purpose, and ensures its place in literature.

NORMANDY, WINTER 2015

Part One

ONE

THE OLDER YOU BECOME, the more a story changes. It takes on layers of wisdom, usually when the people concerned appear to you in dreams after they've died. My father was no fisherman or writer, but because of him I became both. Alive, he haunted the house. It was like being raised by an atmosphere, not by a man. Dead, he haunts my novels, so what more is left to say of him? Well, not only does the story change with age, but the desire for answers is sharper, more insistent.

He was born Glady Win Henry Petley in Wellington, New Zealand, in 1919. He rode a horse to school bareback and attended lessons in bare feet. He learned to steal with his toes, rolled his own smokes behind the playground fence, then left school at thirteen to work as a cabin boy on the lorries. Aged fourteen he presented himself for a job as a driver with a haulage firm. He'd never driven before, just ridden a horse. The foreman told him to hop it, but Glady was chewing tobacco and said he was seventeen, a shaver, and could drive a lorry. So the gaffer told him to get in the seat and prove it.

For a year he'd watched his own gaffers drive. He knew all the moves, he could do the motor maintenance, speak driver's slang. He cranked up the engine with a handle and took the foreman for a faultless turn round the streets of Wellington. The foreman gave him the job and didn't ask to see his papers. I only heard this story once, but it hung over my bed like the shutter on a lantern, regulations on a schoolroom wall. It was, in fact, his one true lesson; the gift of observation.

He drove the lorry for two years, then ran away to sea at sixteen under a false identity, an able-bodied seaman on a merchant ship bound for the world. He became Mac. The real Mac had been a Scot on the SS *Orcades* who jumped ship in Wellington for a sweetheart. Glady swapped his papers and took his place, having never been to sea before.

But the sea runs through it, small islanders all of us. Mac's own father Gladwyn was, as a 12-year-old in 1877, already well known among Auckland yachtsmen for his prowess in sailing small boats. And Mac's grandfather was Hellfire Jack of Tairua, one of the most notorious seamen of his time.

In the Tairua Valley of the late nineteenth century, it was boomtown. A man called Fagan had the bush-felling contract. The men were paid big cheques and spent Friday night in the lock-up. The 'bushmen' and gum diggers worked sixty-hour weeks. The Sash and Door Company sawed day and night till every tree had disappeared, till there were no scows laden with logs on the wharf for the men to admire on Sundays, as they sauntered with their wives. The lucrative cargo of masts and spars which Hellfire Jack had carried were no more.

So Hellfire Jack married a Maori girl and did the 'milk run'. In 1881, a 44-foot cutter was registered under the name of *Half-Caste*. She was designed for speed, to outrun the revenue cutter *Hawk*. Her milk was moonshine from the still at Boat Harbour. Once *Hawk* overtook her, but *Half-Caste* dumped the moonshine into the ocean with a line and float attached. The dodge worked and the revenue men were tricked. *Half-Caste*'s end came when she was blown ashore and wrecked.

Mac went to war, all five years on merchant ships, surviving two torpedoes. His jazz records, and the trumpet Louis Armstrong gave him when sailing home after entertaining the troops, were lost at sea on the return passage. The *Orcades* went down in the Atlantic with a cargo of Chesterfields, tipped. He worked on PLUTO (Pipe Line Under the Ocean) in preparation for D-Day, and became a boatswain. Photos show a lean and sunburned sailor in a grass skirt with his arms round a shipmate after shore leave in the Pacific, or a weary mariner with a dreadnought-grey face while dodging U-boats in Atlantic convoy.

Doreen Josh, or Don, as she was known, was serving in the Gravesend NAAFI when Mac disembarked. Her own father was a Cockney stoker on the Woolwich tugs who'd spent his early years in Hollywood as Pearl White's bellboy. Don and Mac married upriver in Greenwich. A daughter, Lulu, was born just after the war. Mac worked inner London as a taxi driver. Without his vaudeville regulars, it was thin pickings. When Lulu was born he was still in his demob suit, with a pocket full of pawn tickets and coupons. It was petrol off spivs and rations for favours, so he ditched the taxi and bought a 1926 Morris. The Petleys loaded up their belongings, strapped the furniture to the roof and set off for the Weald on the Kent and East Sussex border, to seek their fortune, and to have a son in the country.

They became itinerant, one step behind the gypsies, hawking their labour from farm to farm in the Rother Valley. Newenden, Bodiam, Etchingham, Robertsbridge. In the early 1950s, the Weald was still the Garden of England. The big breweries kept hop farms. The gentleman farmers did well. At its peak, there were seventy thousand acres of hops in Kent and Sussex. Today there might be three thousand, and most of the old hop fields have become vineyards. The family farmer grew soft fruit, all bound for the canning towns of jam and juice. The apples went to market, or into pies and cider.

Mac and Don arrived when hops were still picked by hand. There was labour for able-bodied incomers, from planting to harvest, six months of piece work if you stretched it out. Photos from the period show a happy couple in their early thirties settling into country life: at the front gate of an eighteenth-century tiled cottage, 1950; a picnic on the South Downs when Lulu is five, 1952; Mac leaning on a hoe, Lulu camera-shy between them, Don dressed rather jauntily for the garden, 1950.

When the mud turned cold, and the hop pickers went back to Canning Town themselves, Mac scavenged for work in winter. Don skivvied, Mac fixed vehicles and exterminated pests. He shot crows, poisoned moles, ratted barns, trapped magpies, ferreted rabbits and beat for the guns and redcoats.

By the time I was born in the summer of 1955, the Petleys were living in a council house in Hawkhurst, still a sleepy village off Mr Jones the butcher's A21, halfway between Hastings and Tunbridge Wells, a post-war overspill for demobbed country workers. On my birth certificate, Mac's occupation is *rodent operative*. The new red-brick council estates were a haven for the drifters of 1945, men and women cut loose from pre-war ties by duty, chaos, the scattering of war. Down All Saints Road we had a Welsh miner, a Scottish spinster, an East End boxer and the Kiwi with his Cockney. Mac wasn't the only rat catcher. There were three ex-gamekeepers and enough Land Army women who'd trapped and ratted for victory before going back to boiling their sheets. In fact it was All Saints and Sinners Road; a gypsy family of ten who carved wooden tent pegs, men who worked in the gypsum mine, an engraver, a retired Sheffield tram driver, a chimney sweep, a nurseryman, estate gardeners laid off on the eve of war, bus drivers, dustmen, coalmen, milkmen, widows and wounded. There were craftsmen too, cobblers, watch repairers, furniture makers. But most were labourers: on local farms where the tied cottages were being sold off; at the wood turners beside the railway station where they made the hop poles; or just chippies, brickies and plasterers for the new 'gentlemen' builders. The women worked in the village shops, the laundry or the egg-packing plant. Or, like Don, they did seasonal work on the fruit farms and skivvied for the district's burgeoning middle classes. The aristocracy had fled, their mansions left empty after housing convalescing troops. Their estates were divided into farmland or secured for the new council estates. All Saints Road, Park Cottages, Basden, Wellington Cottages, Red Oaks. In secure housing at low rent, the idea was that working families could settle down in rural tranquillity and prosper under the new Welfare State. But not the Macs of this world. The bitterness of poverty and stifling hierarchies on foreign soil had begun to set Mac against himself.

As an immigrant, he didn't fully identify with the English rural working man, to live without respect from local gentry and the jumped-up squires who employed the men. The Sheriff of Kent had been a Petley in the 1500s, and the court in Tonbridge was named after him. At Battle, where William the Conqueror's men had defeated King Harold's army in 1066, there is Petley Wood. Old England was steeped in Petleys, only they'd ended up on convict ships or keeping the peace with the Irish Guards in the new colonies.

Don had never considered this, that when a man comes to his mother country he expects recognition. The eldest of nine, Don's own father was proud to have Bow Bells ringing in his ears. Don spoke wistfully of pease pudd'n and faggots, jellied eels, the Pearly King and Queen of distant relation. Mac remembered the mechanical. There were no people, no family on his lips. On Don's mother's side, there were travelling folk, show people of the fairgrounds. Her maiden name was Josh, about as onomatopoeic an English working-class surname as you can get. A Petley was a pit lea, a shithole, a field latrine, a pit in a lea.

Mac's split with human nature had already taken place after he entered service for Lord Curzon's widow, the Marchioness of Keddlestone, at the Bodiam Castle Dower House in 1950. Mac as chauffeur/handyman, Don as mop and duster. The drunken cook of spurned advances had sabotaged the boilers one night ensuring Mac would take the blame. Shithole and Josh were turned out on the spot. Lady Curzon discovered the truth sometime later and invited them back. Mac tore the letter into shreds. The Marchioness sold up and returned to her seat up North. This left no room in Mac's heart for compassion and negotiation.

My earliest memory is of standing with Mac in a field in winter, cold wet grass and mole hills on a slope. I'm three. Below us is the River Rother. A steam train makes its way along the valley to Etchingham. Behind me, Mac is killing moles. Later, he takes me to the edge of a wood to show me a long row of his dead crows, strung from post to post by their eye sockets.

His split with actual nature came with *Lulubelle*, a white Austin 7 Tourer built in 1930, registration OT 3101. Her long bonnet opened like a bird in flight, her bolted-eye headlamps you could cradle in your arms like geese. Wings swept down on to a running-board where two brass-capped Redline cans painted blue were strapped with brass-buckled leather tack. The flat glass windscreen opened outwards. A velvet blind with silk tassels pulled down over the back window. The seats were like deep leather armchairs. Onlookers clapped as we drove past. A rook and caw from the hooter made them cheer. Most of All

Saints Road just laughed at another old Petley banger.

Mac couldn't create himself, but he'd found his state of being, his passover into matter, metal, junk. *Lulubelle* was the first of many. Family life sacrificed, dedicated to the restoration of the vintage motor car. Mac spent his spare life under *Lulubelle*, hours after dark, lit by a streetlamp. Our weekends were wasted touring breakers' yards, Mac's rainy evenings indoors chasing up enthusiasts from their adverts in *Motor Sport*. Eccentric men in leather caps and goggles came and went. Men with long, posh names sent the dog into a frenzy. Their low resonant voices made the windows rattle. Silk cravats and red necks which made Don tut and scorn. They all turned up in some sleek roadster from the jazz age boulevards and race tracks; Mr Twallin in a Silver Ghost, Paul Foulkes-Halbard in an open-topped Bugatti.

They left Don banging saucepans together in the sink when Mac went for a spin. But something clawed him back to us, before he drifted away for good. Probably Don, sobbing in the kitchen as another lump of oily British metal lay on sheets of the *Daily Express* under her cooker. All too briefly, that boy who'd once ridden bareback to school and then come to this dark-grey, post-war land in another hemisphere, had something to pass on to us, after all. One summer morning in 1959, he woke us an hour before dawn and drove us deep in to the dark of Bedgebury Forest. We'd gone there, he said, to watch the sun rise.

He packed the billy can and spirit stove and he fried sausages and eggs and bread in a blackened pan. The sun rose on the baked yellow track and threw shadows over ant hills, under pines tall as the sky. It was like walking on the moon, the world no one saw, the breakfasts only Petleys had ever tasted. We repeated this ritual every Sunday, all that summer. Maybe Mac was showing us the life he'd given up, like time was running out for him. One minute he was open, helping us along the right fork in the path, the next minute he was shut, a foreigner who'd left his past sealed in a black box down under. The land he'd settled in had nothing to offer, just the unwanted cars of its own past.

He found them under tarpaulins, in barns, dilapidated coach houses, weeded-up yards at the backs of run-down garages, places which became his domain. He smelt out vintage cars like he smelt a rat. A handful of change to a widow, a few hours clipping the hedge, fixing a gutter, smoking out some wasps, and the old crate was his. The gift brought inert machinery to life, a gift which stifled the living, turned our life back to machinery. Without knowing it, he'd become an Englishman. The amateur, the enthusiast, a player against gents, a place where he could share a pitch and bowl with the toffs, where the autodidact is admired while he creates a living widow. The barefoot rider had been extinguished. By then, he was naturalised British, neutralised Kiwi. His accent was gone. The past was a foreign land.

He drove to work in a suit now. A rent collector for the council. Don wore slippers and housecoats and complained of bunions and loneliness. Lulu was thirteen and lived in her room with a transistor radio. It was like the family had split up in the same house. Life was a running repair; everything was a bother when Mac came home. Then one Saturday morning in June 1960, something happened. He came through the back door with a fishing rod instead of a headache.

TWO

IT CAME FROM THE VILLAGE SWEET SHOP, where it must have lain for thirty years. A fishing rod, suddenly shining in the sunlight on our dining-room table, so pretty in its red silk whippings. Mottled cane smooth under yacht varnish, a bottle-green wooden handle, sliding brass reel fittings, a rubber button on the end of the butt. Don scowled at it, suspicious and put out. Another perishing thing. The coming of the fishing rod into a family like ours spelled its doom, and she knew it.

In my eyes it was another of those mystery objects from the grown-up universe. It joined the striped hatbox, the monkey wrench, a girdle, the cannon-ball in the shed, the bos'n's whistle, my dead uncle's letters wrapped in a blue silk handkerchief tied up with red ribbon, the First World War pistol under a cardigan in Mac's desk; evocative objects which appeared in nightmares once you touched them.

To Mac the rod was expense. Expense meant he'd met someone he needed to impress. Bruce would put him on to something. This was why we were going roach fishing with Bruce. Mr Pullen at the sweet shop had told Mac it was a boy's rod, and boys caught roach. Mac called it a Hong Kong lawyer. Stiff as a hop pole, eyes like key rings, two-piece, seven-feet long, it was only fit for quelling riots and yanking pot-jacks out of meres, not roach from the River Rother.

The East Sussex Rother was three miles south of Hawkhurst. I'd only seen it in winter colours. One Sunday afternoon, we'd stood in the lane below Burgh Hill at Etchingham, gazing over the fields with plastic telescopes and Brownie cameras. The black family saloons, polished and Turtle Waxed, all parked in a row along the hedge. Their glad-raggers had come to gloat at a river in flood, in extravagant flow and not about to suffer fools gladly. It was a troublesome river, the bane of English kings for centuries. In those days you went to visit the Rother Valley floods of a Sunday afternoon, to feast your eyes on the drowned landscape like it was a sick aunt.

The water came all the way up to the five-bar gate. Oilskin tourists waded across or swooped down on bikes into brown water deeper than wellington tops. I clung to the landlubbers. My scanty knowledge of horror swelled in that flood, and the nightmares began; I stood alone in fields of flat calm sick on all sides. One move and I drown in the migrating sea, no warning line of bankside trees spell out the river within. For thirty years I shall have that Rother dream. Like a memory of the dead, the river only sleeping, its wrinkles smoothed in a spreading repose. It stops only when I learn to swim.

Our first fishing trip was to Etchingham, the very place of dream. On a June afternoon, in a stiff summer breeze, I walked down a grassy slope to an old dappled river. As the men fished, I gazed down windswept water, a gaze which burned itself into a memory. Framed like a landscape painting, one of the few chosen by a growing consciousness to keep for the deathbed. It was important, I knew it too, but I was alone and the river flowed by without me.

Mac fished standing up, rod skyward, moaning by the minute, trying to grab his hook as the wind sent it whiplashing out of reach. Bruce sat downstream on his wicker basket, stock still beside an alder, his orange quill riding the current. Mac couldn't get his bread to stay on the hook, so he pinched a sultana out of our scones and nicked it on the point. It fooled a one-minute roach, a silver leaf spinning in the wind. I had met the first wonder of my world.

Our last trip was in November. The Hexden Channel down from Newenden. The memory is more insistent and nervous now. The cold dark-green grass, the first thick winter muds, the hewing wind across our bobble hats. Mac tried two half-hearted casts then handed me the rod out of spite, with no instruction. So this was it, the first touch of the rod in the boy's hand. A wind knot in the line kinked into a bird's nest. The rod blew out of my clutches before the float came out of the sky.

'Nay goot,' Mac said. 'Pack it in.'

Bruce stayed catching live bait for jack pike and never asked us again. Back home, our gear was dumped under the bench in the shed behind the dog's box, and forgotten.

THREE

ONE DAY IN THE SUMMER HOLIDAYS when I was ten, a boy called Kevin Spice from up the road simply said:

'You got a fishing rod, incha, Dex?'

Kevin Spice, with his unsoiled tackle and crisp new clothes, made everything he did look deliberate and mechanical. The rest of us improvised in hand-me-downs and chaos. His family were recent arrivals down All Saints Road, aloof and private, snob-fearing. It was like they'd sent Kevin out to convert us. His perfection was part of Spice family aura, living as they did in the highest, most inaccessible house on the estate, up a long concrete path, atop a high brick wall. The clean and sober Spices were as upright as Methodists, but their snobbery was heathen. Kevin's beautiful tackle was matched by his brother's, their shiny bikes and department-store toys a carefully nurtured difference schooled rigidly by their father, a plasterer with a Hastings building contractor. To deliver their sense of superiority, they employed what to us was strange and radical humour, back-slang and American accents, parodies of TV Westerns, puns and impressions. Their ordinary conversation was vaudeville. It made us doubt ourselves, we who spoke directly in our own tongue, which until Kevin and his elder brother descended among us had never let us down. Yet there I was, trembling in fear and awakening before this younger boy because he'd divined I owned a long-forgotten fishing rod.

'Yeah, I 'ave,' I said, like it was a scene from *Sleeping Beauty*.

'We're going down Ockley Pool,' he said. 'Go git yer rod, gib loof.'

The flowering rod was where we'd left it, curiously preserved, memories of the Rother intact. And still in wait beside it, an Oxo tin of sundries inside a gas-mask haversack, a tiny Milbro tray of split shot, a packet of hooks to nylon in a booklet of greaseproof-paper envelopes sown at the spine, a dumpy cork and balsa perch float ringed like a schoolboy's cap. The rod was still tackled up with the same old twenty-five yards of nylon line on the maroon, bird-scarer reel. I even fancied the dried bogey on the hook was the remains of that sultana.

I remember Kevin's tackle to this day too, because it impressed me with its obvious access to knowledge and ritual, something I'd missed in 1960. So unlike Mac's sweet-shop poker, I wanted to run my fingers over it, impatient to learn what the curious shapes and auras of this tackle meant. Kevin's rod was an eight-foot, solid-glass, blind-eye coloured fly rod, his reel an Intrepid Black Prince which he said was made of monkey metal. With a banana-shaped goose quill float and the evenly spaced split shot, his whole kit formed the shape, as he carried it so expertly pointing backwards, of a violin bow or a cut-throat blade. It seemed so deadly, musical and efficient. Such grace and fervour needed a destination worthy of this intent. Hawkhurst had just the place in Ockley Pool.

Even the journey to Ockley Pool was charged with anticipation. Along the High Street, the colonnade of shops became a caravanserai for boys off to war like armed trekkers, swishing rods for all occasions. True coming of age is when you go fishing that first time on your own. And there is nothing like a hunting party to announce the arrival of your soul to a few shopkeepers. We traversed the entire village, past Piper's the newsagent's, Baldock's the baker's, The Wool Shop, the tobacconist's, the chemist's, turned right at the laundry into Cranbrook Road, past the antiques shop, forking into Ockley Lane at the Bandbox, cooing at the manikins, *haute couture* and lace frillies for country women, Kevin leading us on into the subverted world of Spice:

''Ere, Gibbon, arse me where me dad's bin this week.'

'Where?'

'No, not Ware, Hoo.'

'But you said where.'

'No I didn't, he was in Ware last week. Yesterday he went to Hoo. You're such a gib loof, Hoss. Y'ain goan ketch no creek critter, is 'e Rexted?'

And so it must have gone, Kevin twisting his tongue until I was 'Rexted', his cousin Wayne 'Gibbon', and Gibbon's brother Vincent became 'Skinny'. The more Kevin attacked our language and ventriloquised our identities, the closer we came to what I wanted to be.

Beside Pullen's sweets and tackle, my rod showed no emotion other than pressing onward behind the boasting of tacticians. We may have paused and leaned our rods outside, like horses at the inn, to purchase penny chews or a bottle of Vimto, but I do not remember. I just recall the hypnotic sight of the float bouncing up and down in stride, the sense that this excitement pulling me forward was brand new, a breached frontier as important as new teeth, long trousers, or playing kiss chase in the playground and discovering that Felicity Stapley had let me catch her under the beech tree.

As we left the last houses behind, we plunged down a stone track towards a faint roar in the valley below. Trees on a high bank touched the sky, great ruts and channels where the rain had coursed down over centuries made us stumble, till at the bottom we came to an old, overgrown bridge, a sag in the wire fence and over we went, plunging down a well-worn path, naturally stepped between the tree roots. And there, like an adventure comic palace, was the secret of Ockley Pool.

To miniature explorers, it was a play-sized Owen Falls. Instead of the source of the Nile, it was the source of many a Hawkhurst boy's piscatorial curse. The unforgettable scent of wild garlic, the ozone of thrashing water, drumming underground as it thumped against stone. For such a tiny water-course, two hops across downstream, it punched above its depth. The waterfall itself was only two-feet high, the stream rushing under the lane and tumbling from a Victorian stone-walled tunnel, out on to dark-green boulders. From there it swept past oblong slabs of grey stone. These formed the right-hand bank, which opened out to create an oval pool no more than thirty feet wide and fifty feet long. But to us, it was as long as the day is pure, or as short as your patience for a swiftly moving float.

The whole pool was tucked from sight, shaded in by trees. Shafts of sunlight pierced where able. Some fell on the water under the opposite bank. Here the roots of an oak pushed against the return eddy. Clumps of brambles and a barbed-wire fence made access there look tricky and wild. A slack spiral in the lower pool turned slowly over tan-coloured silt. Here the sticks and parcels of leaves washed up and ran aground.

I watched the others set their floats an arm's length deep and cast their worms with underarm flicks. Red and yellow tips raced towards swirling boils, dipping in the peat-brown water, floats dancing within a thousand bubbles, or pulling under on the shallows as they swung in at the end of their run, shipwrecked against half-submerged stones, moss-green and shining.

My maiden cast took place at the foot of the pool. Like Mac on his gaffers, I'd observed the others so closely, though the fishing slang and the tackle maintenance were yet to come. At least the feared ridicule remained unspoken. We were just four boys fishing a pool four-boys wide, the roar of the water plugging out all other sound, the living tips of our floats consuming our entire field of vision.

Under the kind of tutelage you only get from your mates, or the drip-dry Kevins of this world, I learned to fish that day, learned to fish with a sense of urgency. It was life's first great lesson in who I would become, in states of being and codes of conduct, on watercraft, observation, independence, emotion, philosophy. Inch by inch, that first hour, the circumference of my float widened, and I began to pull more line off the little red reel, urging my float to take risks and swim the perilous and uncharted passage, instead of circling at my fishless feet. I learned both from experience and frequent sly glances at the others. I unpicked tangles, squeezed on split shot with my teeth, unhooked sticks and leaves, grasped the knack of keeping a worm going. I noticed Kevin's many attempts to flick his worm under the far bank, but his float was snatched away in the current before it arrived. Rather than relinquish his prime spot at the turbulent head of the pool, he continued to ply the middle ground, while insisting the big 'uns were under the far bank, where crimson roots glimmered in the sparkling water. I fished rooted to the shallow end, as Ockley Pool appeared eternally deep, but was probably no more than four feet, shallowing up to eighteen inches at the tail of the pool before it compressed into a shallow rapid and headed for Mick the Pig's scrapyard.

After only an hour as a fisherboy, I realised my best chance of a bite was on that far side. Kevin had hooked a four-inch brown trout on his second cast. It had shown briefly in the air then flipped off as he swung it in. But now his float plucked and shuddered each run down until his shout of 'Got one!' produced another tiny six-inch brown trout, this time shimmying into his hand.

His boasting began to spill over into derision, so I made my move, slipping over the mossy slabs, jumping a tiny inlet which trickled in where the main current hit clay and cut left for another twenty feet. Wagtails dipped up and down at the foot of the pool, picking off flies which rose from the troubled surface. I wore my wellingtons folded over at the top, like a pirate or smuggler. The shallows were no match for them and I pushed up on to the other bank, clearing my way through brambles and bushes. I remember the struggle to get that float into water, the line snagging on blackberry whips and my fear of looking a fool now that I was directly opposite the others and in Kevin's critical line of vision. And yet they knew I had never fished before. They were already four-season anglers, but they still snagged the bottom or the trees behind them. If they jeered at me, I never heard them over the roar of the water.

The moment came when my float shuddered and was gone. Its tip paled, helpless underwater. I tugged it back and snatched up a plucky six-inch brown trout of my own. The others saw it, and I was one of them. It became the smell of childhood from then on; that dry snaky slime, like the painted smell of its thousand-coloured spots on pinhead scales, punging in the back of the nose.

Ockley Pool itself always made you feel it was your secret alone. The place was grateful because you put its fishes back. The place was generous because it let you catch them again. You climbed in, like into a lost country, but when you climbed back out to go home, you felt as if you were returning from slipped time.

I never went fishing with proud Kevin again, but the cane rod became a constant companion, fumbling fish from pool, pond and ditch, converting sweets and comics on pocket-money day into further rash tackle acquisitions from Pullen's.

Ma Pullen ran the shop with her son Mike. Sweets, pop, toys, Frog and Airfix kits, air pistols, pocket knives and fishing tackle. A cramped, bow-fronted, white weatherboard corner shop from the Just William stories. Fresh green paint, a bell over the door, the smell of tea kettles from behind the flowered curtain where old Ma Pullen waited beside a miser's hoard of toasted teacakes, gold-coated from molten butter. She served the sweets from jars and weighed them on a balance with her stack of brass avoirdupois. She wore floral dresses from her days as a dance band piano player, now slippered and lipsticked, hunched under a shawl. Her bearded son did the toys and tackle. A bachelor boy, red checked shirts and elbow-patched cardigans, thick-rimmed spectacles, a stale chapel aura which we probably confused with lack of ambition or motherly suffocation. He was no fisherman, worse luck for him, but he had the patience and the organisation: everything in Oxo tins or biscuit tins, pike floats in sweet jars, sundries in shallow wooden drawers, all labelled and put back afterwards. I can only imagine how he longed to gather up his wares, take them down the river and never come back.

Why we trusted him to guide us in our requirements is more to do with childhood's desire to fish than Pullen sharking us. Half the boys of Hawkhurst fished for roach with either a sea-boat rod or a fly rod, due to Pullen's ignorant stocking policy or dishonest travellers in tackle. All the clues we needed for selecting a proper rod were readily available in books for fisherboys, like *Mr Crabtree Goes Fishing*. We all had a volume. Yet I still purchased the five-foot solid glass, wooden-handled sea-boat rod because Mr Pullen said it was a pike rod. He was sincere and authoritative, till we outgrew his bluffing. Until we saw a real pike rod, we believed him. But on its own, even the best fishing rod is a dead stick. There has to be a magician, the coming of a genuine rodsmith to push the object onward, into imagination; someone whose example you remember in the nick of time twenty years later.

FOUR

I WAS ELEVEN WHEN I BEGAN to notice Mr Cavey, the man who lived next door in number forty-nine. Known by everyone as Doug, he rode a BSA Bantam 125 with a leopard-skin saddle cover, the gear change modified to accommodate a tin leg. He'd lost his real leg in the war while serving in the motorcycle Army Dispatch Corps. By the 1950s, the need for old-style gamekeepers like him died out when the estates were dismantled and the mansions pulled down. Doug and Edna had three sons and a cocker spaniel, the gun dog Lady. She travelled pillion, sitting upright in an open-topped, green wooden box. The sign on the Caveys' pea-green front door said: *KV PRODUCTS, Leather Goods, Shooting & Fishing Accessories.*

They lived upside down. Doug's workshop was downstairs where the front room should have been. Television and tea was upstairs in the new front room. The council didn't like it, not least when every spring he turned number forty-nine into a trout and salmon hatchery. The bathroom was put out of bounds and several thousand trout and salmon eggs hatched in the bath tub, from fry-tank to stock-pond size. In the backyard, under the kitchen window, he dug a three-feet-deep pond, installed a circulating pump and wired it over. In went the fingerlings, dry fed for half a year. He released them as rainbow trout yearlings a brace at a time into the lakes at Slip Mill and Risden. From Slip Mill they leaked into the Hexden stream and we caught them on worms as far down as Ockley Pool.

One day I caught an eight-incher below Slip Mill and took it home wrapped in a dock leaf, then hung about the front hedge till Mr Cavey came down his garden path. I'd decided it was about time he knew I went fishing.

He winked at me and clicked his tongue.

'Ello, bin fish'n', tharn? Any joy?'

'Yeah, cawt this.'

I put the trout on the hedge and he creaked down for a butcher's. He shook his head sadly.

'Tut tut, should'na killed that. Way undersized, and I'm sure it's one o' me rainbers. Where d'yer ketchit?'

'Down the Dump,' I said.

He knew a fisherman's lie when he heard one.

I spent months trying to worm my way back to his attention, convinced he would accept me as a brother of the angle and take me fishing if he saw I wasn't just next door's kid who'd poached one of his rainbows. I spread my fishing gear all over the lawn, hung my net to dry in the ivy, dug worms all day, put them back and dug them up again. He never fell for it. When he came out, he just ignored me and went on his way.

As he was a fly fisherman, I pretended to be a fly fisherman too. I swished my rod about in the back garden sending imaginary flies over the hedge. Mr Cavey failed to rise. Instead, the tip section flew off and put a crack in his kitchen window. So I gave him up and got on with the actual fishing. We were in different worlds. Men in Barbours, Norfolk tweeds and deerstalkers knocked on his door. *Trout & Salmon* magazine ran a centre-page feature on his breeding: TROUT FARM IN A COUNCIL HOUSE.

He gave up fish breeding not long after this, keeping a few rainbows and one brown trout in his garden pond. From my bed I listened to him feed them at night. At ten-thirty, his backdoor creaked open. He called his spaniel with two clicks of the tongue. His tin leg creaked and the steel tips of his Veldtschoens rang on the concrete path as he took his usual turn, sniffed the air, looked at the sky, pulled the cover over his Bantam. The warm, still nights were best. I would sneak to the window and listen. He would fetch a blood-wet polythene bag of defrosted liver chunks, clear his throat, then flip the liver chunk by chunk on the water, a mash of trout foam as they ripped it with their needle teeth, gouging swirls like a downpour as the spaniel whined at heel. Man and beast, the way they slowed the world and gave my imagination the slip.

These were sacred minutes for which I stayed awake, to share with them all, man, spaniel and trout. I would kneel at the open window squinting into the dark, trying to see what they were doing. Why so still, so silent? What was I craving for in that nothingness? It was all beyond me, so I just accepted they were lingering out there with the six fish circling each other in the liver-blood slicks. Old Hop-Along, half lit from the bare light bulb in his window, until his bulky shadow limped over the water, a fraction before the light was extinguished. I couldn't fall asleep until then.

One night I decided go out there and capture the moment for myself, be Mr Cavey, steal the secret of man and fish. When Don thought I was having my weekly wash in the kitchen sink before bed, I snipped the corner off tomorrow's liver and crept up the back garden in the dark. I lobbed the liver over the hedge at Hop-Along's pond. No splash, nothing. I had no dog. There was no moon. It was a chilly autumn evening. I'd forgotten about the fine chicken-wire pond cover, there to stop falling leaves fouling the clear water. The liver must have stuck on it. Then some bloody water dripped off the liver. There was one listless swirl, then another until they were lashing at the wire, half a dozen trout about two pounds each throwing themselves at the mesh right under the Caveys' kitchen window.

One night in October there was a knock at the door. Martin, the youngest Cavey, asked for me. His dad thought I might like to see a fish he'd caught. This was so out of the blue I suspected he was out to catch me. But the fish was there, laid out on their kitchen table, like someone in the family had died. It was huge, the biggest fish I'd ever seen.

'Well,' he said winking, 'd'yer know what she is, then?'

'Salmon,' I said.

'Sea trout, lad, sea trout. Nine-and-a-half-pound she is. Caught 'er down Udj'm, in the Rother there. Is'n she a beauty?'

The Rother at Udiam was just a small brown stream under an old bridge.

'Ow did I ketch 'er?' he said to himself. 'Oorn a spinner. Saw 'er goo whoosh a coupl'a toimes. She grabbed it first chuck.'

He showed me the rod and reel. Hardy ten-foot hollow-glass salmon spinning rod and an Intrepid Elite fixed-spool reel, a spoon of burnished gold and silver with red wool trailing and still wet on a treble hook. He winked as he let me out the front door. The only man I've ever known who winked.

Another slow and winkless winter set in. He was off on his Bantam with his shotgun, a KV Products game bag, Lady the Spaniel sitting upright in the green wooden pillion box. Next day there would be a brace of pheasant hung outside their back door, or a duck, or rabbits. Come spring and he was away with his trout rod tied to his back with hop string. Then the smell of baking trout rose over the hedge, game bag hanging out to air on that game nail by their back door.

Number forty-nine was always busy. They kept their front door open all day, and the smell of leather and dog and fur always worked its way across our hedge. The sound of growing lads thumping up and downstairs, the treadles in the workshop, Mr Cavey clearing his throat. It was like they threw their house open for an illustration in a school encyclopaedia, a cutaway drawing of happiness and industry with all its rooms inside out and everything labelled. The rest of All Saints Road was parlours and net curtains, and not a peep from the Petley Chapel of Rest, in case it gave Don one of her headaches. And all the while, up and down the Caveys' front path, came all these men, women and children with their cartridge belts, handbags, gun bags, game bags, braces, watchstraps, satchels and briefcases. Douglas Cavey was the peoples' mender. From his hard-up neighbours, the coalman's jerkin, the down-at-heel spinster's suitcase, to the tall countrymen in brogues and cravats with their Pall Mall rod cases, the front door opened on them all.

One afternoon I was sent round there myself with Don's handbag. One of the seams needed stitching. Mr Cavey was dressing flies in his workshop. He said I would never be a fisherman until I could tie a fly. So that was it then. I was not a fisherman. My roach were too lowly.

I learned quickly under his tuition. After an hour I could tie a plausible nymph, a March Brown, a Greenwell's Glory. He gave me an old fly-tying vice, a thick cardboard box of assorted dressings, even a very used wet fly line to be going on with. I already had a fly rod, of sorts. Mike Pullen, at the height of his powers, had fooled me into parting with thirty bob for a six-foot split-cane boat rod which converted to a nine-foot fly rod. At last, there in his sanctum, I asked Mr Cavey the question I had saved up for nearly two years:

'Can I come fishin' wiv you up Risden?'

'No, lad,' he said.

I was thirteen. All I wanted in life was to catch tench and rudd. Mr Cavey couldn't allow this, and attempted to convert me from it. All the adventure of riding pillion on his Bantam, clinging to his thickened leather waist, fell flat on a trip to Darwell Reservoir instead, a fly-only sea of trout. Just the calm patches were as big as any pond I knew. It was like Mac taking me to the races at Brands Hatch, only to find it was motorbikes and not cars. As the flies hatched in the June afternoon, my heart sank just knowing there were real fish in this reservoir, forbidden fish you were not allowed to mention. Mr Cavey said the only chance that day was out in the boat, but for my benefit we flogged nymphs off the east bank a hundred yards apart. He waded down the concrete slope, water up to his thighs. I cast into mirrors in the hot stagnant margins, the sun glaring back at me. I didn't even see a trout rise on the whole million acres. Every cast, I hooked a pair of startled eyes. My nymph was their first meal. Hop-Along said I must kill them, but I slipped them back on the sly. They were my kind of fish, those budling perch.

About four o'clock there was a yelling. I threw the rod down and legged it along the bank thinking he'd hooked a big one. He had his tin leg firmly wedged in a crevice, still inside a wader, water up to his pockets. He was a stout heavy man not used to balancing acts.

'Run down the weighin' hut,' he said. 'Fetch Ted or Sammy up here, and doan be long.'

They both held Hop-Along under the arms so he could unstrap his leg. Then they hauled him up the bank and hoiked his leg out with a boat hook. I carried on whisking for perch as he sat on his jacket and dried his empty trouser.

Some evenings, he still came down the front path with his fly rod on his back, bound for the evening rise up Risden. I was that kid next door again, the one who caught the blunt common roach from russet farm ponds. He might wink and swing his head, or he might not, but each time now his square face remained impassive, hard-lined, fissures in a drought. Perhaps his leg was rubbing his stump. Perhaps hair turning steel-grey hurt as it turned. Then he would stand by his Bantam, talking to himself in that burred, throtteral voice, as if I were not there:

'Oh dear,' he said. 'Oh dear, oh dear, oh dear.'

I would hold my breath till he kick-started the Bantam and wheeled it to the kerb. Then everything was on course again, like he'd never said those words. I carried on fishing the village ponds with stale bread and no heart in it, while Hop-Along went up Risden on those balmy evenings. All day I would ask myself why, why couldn't he take me there, just once?

Risden was a private estate lake two miles outside the village. Hop-Along had sole rights and fished it alone. I'd caught delicious glimpses of it through the trees from the bus window, and I knew there were tench and lily pads, probably a boathouse; everything, in fact, that I considered life was about. I even had a blank page reserved for it in my *Fishing Log Book*. But me and Hop-Along just weren't in sympathy. There was something about him coming through like a weak signal. Maybe it was the truth about fishing, the one he was so reluctant to pass on.

In turn, I became equally reluctant to attract his attention. If I dared, he would stop mid-stride, close his eyes painfully, then limp with awful resignation over to the fence. He would cup his hand over one ear and I'd repeat my question.

'Hmmmm? Rizden? Come again, lad?'

One evening, he was coming down the long, sloping concrete path from his front door, trout bag, net and rod in hand, boot nails from his tin foot sparking. He saw me there, but walked straight through my shadow with his own. He pushed the Bantam between his front gate posts, upped it on to its stand, stood in thought, then pivoted round and said:

'I'm going up Rizden, lad. If you can be ready in five minutes I'll take you along. Just your rod, net and haversack, mind.'

At Field Green he stood the Bantam beside a five-bar gate and we set off down the field towards a clump of trees at the bottom. A fence ran along the length of pine trees. A nye of pheasant fretted away. Wood pigeons cluttered through the branches. We were close now. A sign on a tree said KEEP OUT. PRIVATE. NO FISHING. I climbed the stile, he unlocked a gate. We pushed through undergrowth, and there it was, Risden Lake, like a sunrise in the night. We were in one corner where the path emerged on to the dam. It was the most beautiful lake I had ever seen.

Tunnels in the rhododendrons twisted into gaps as far as the shallows where a spring ran in through bog and great sedge, rush beds shiring in the wind, clishing in the back breeze. Here the water rippled in sunlight. Elsewhere it stayed black and still. The other bank was open but for one toppled beech tree with its limbs lopped, the grass shin-high, a gently sloping barley field pushing up to the fence. The dam was on the southern bank, where the overflow shoggled through a leaf grate and down the steep embankment into the chestnut wood below.

The estate was now farmland. A French family had owned the country house for three generations. It ended its days housing troops during World War Two, then stood empty till demolition in 1956. The stable block and clock tower remained, saved by a preservation order. Somewhere over the brow was the farmyard, but it was like we were the only anglers in the world.

Even then, when summer skies were long and flat and blue, and life was a choice of ponds from dawn to dusk, or an expedition to a stream, just standing beside Risden introduced a new standard of contentment. So far-reaching, there was danger in the precocious. It rendered childhood an impotent time. It diminished all other water to scum-slicks and public dumps.

Mr Cavey didn't share my delirium. He made it a philosophy to be defended. He pointed to a corner of the dam and said *Fish there and keep out of my way.* My swim was dark and grassless, cold and sterile from the solid shade of rhododendrons. I watched him swish his Hardy Palakona on the open bank where the water seemed blue and the sun shone on the swaying rushes. I fished where the tench fouled the bottom; he fished where his rainbows swam in sunlight and oxygen.

I soon forgot him, for the evening was short. The boy will pass up all other wonders of the world for a plate of tench bubbles round his float. I don't recall how many tench I caught. Not more than half a dozen; the biggest might have been 1lb 10ozs, but this was fishing like I'd never known, unsullied by Mr Cavey's scorn for a fish which mucked up the water and made his rainbows cough and pale. It was the last time he ever took me fishing, the last time he considered us brothers of the angle. Like Mac, the heyday of his world shut down and pushed him out of reach.

The 1970s put an end to KV Products. The world went plastic. Handbags, fishing bags, game bags, shotgun cartridge belts, golf bags, all on the cheap and narrow, the plastic of obsolescence for the never-never generation. The smell of leather and canvas over the front hedge was gone. Mr Cavey registered as disabled and Remploy had him put their labels on his own handbags, like prisoners and mental patients. A van came once a month to take his products to a warehouse. They ended up in gift shops. The Bantam was replaced by a Bonneville and sidecar. The spaniel died. He took up things he was no good at, painting by numbers, scenes of rural life, gundogs, shire horses, a rising trout, oil-paint contortions across a sheet of hardboard. 'Doug's Nature Notes' in the free ads paper, the occupational therapy of redundant idylls dreamed up in a rundown workshop, fields and streams remembered like names on a memorial.

After two of the boys left home, Mr Cavey spent his evenings in The Cricketers, a weatherboard, oak-beamed pub where Hawkhurst casualties gathered at the drink. Edna took her driving test. Doug was her 'disabled' passenger now. By 1972 it was like we had never known each other. We never spoke. We became two ex-fishermen who gave up at the same time. The last two trout circled each other under the kitchen window like the final scene in a Spaghetti Western. He hung the KEEP OUT. NO FISHING sign on his heart of oak.

If there is to be any fruitful exchange between man and boy and fishing rod, it has to work both ways, all ways. The last time we spoke I was fifteen, off to Delmonden, one of those farm ponds where wooden carp shapes hung under the surface on hot days, uncatchable wild fish too wise for any of us. I must have caught Mr Cavey on the back cast that day, or the mist had cleared. He walked over to the fence at the sound of 'Delmonden'. The knots in his face unravelled and he spoke of happier days. Summer evenings in the 1950s when he would cast his floating crust in the margins there, hidden behind the reeds till a great wide mouth shlooped down his bait and fought longer and wilder than any sea trout he had ever known. He made those shlooping sounds with his mouth and puppets of his hands. One was a crust, the other a great gob of some old carp devouring the other. For this brief moment he was someone whose existence he had forgotten. And then the show was over. Separating hands, he went back up the sloping concrete path and shut the front door behind him. He'd done the deed, passed the mystery of happiness on before it soured, no matter how distasteful it might have been to him. It was up to me now.

This book is dedicated to him, Douglas Cavey, the true martyr of the rod.

FIVE

ONCE, THERE WAS A TIME so brief, so delicate, you wondered what it was for, the way you wonder at a mayfly whose gift of flight is useless. Within a day it's spent, blown into a graveyard by the wind. Such was time for the fishing boy. Only once, just before it caught the wind, time almost stood still.

In the stillness of 1968 we fished, with the innocent certainty of thieves who have only sipped from the top, too busy cooking our own books to notice the obvious, that the world was changing around us. Carefree days are always on the eve of war; the spoil and disruption on the way is unimaginable. Just as we were learning to live with childhood, making sense of nature, testing links between give and take, it was moribund. We drove a road through it, superseded our margin of error, mutated into ugly, broken-voiced failures, entered a pecking order modelled on borstal, denied we were ever children. But for the moment, while still on its edge, our aim was true. For us, 1968 wasn't a year of protest. We knew nothing of grievance yet. A year was four lifetimes of acceptance, four intricate seasons in a village still ruled by seasons, uncomplicated by desire and knowledge.

Fishing absorbed all of our activities. Each was a gateway to the other, our days ticked off a shepherd's calendar, our decisions bound by folklore. A fickle boy with a decision to make put a wet finger to the wind, observed the cows lying down, the weathervane on the church steeple, the rain gauge, the evening sky. Fishing, football or a trek up the sewer stream looking for old bottles? It was all to play for. We observed Ash Wednesday, took our twigs to school and stamped on the feet of those who hadn't; we reverently obeyed the closed season, switching to April's trout with the ten-inch limit engraved upon our fishing rulers. We attended Sunday school and harvest festival, Guy Fawkes and conker championships, the circus, the fair and the village fête with an equal sense of parish duty. There was a time and place for everything, and each diurnal constant enshrined a village custom: fish and chip van, Friday; cricket, Wednesday; youth club, Monday.

For the moment, we knew who and where we were. Kent boys, the parish wildlife. Foragers, fishers, scrumpers and poachers. Field craft had scant intellectual rigour; we were born into it like cubs with the dirt round our eyes, dirt which came off Sunday nights in a tin bath from a boiling kettle. Our pockets were full of string and hops, chestnuts, rose hips, lucky rabbit tails, sheep's teeth. Our dads had fox tails hanging from their rear views. Our heads measured time in tench bubbles and cuckoo spit. We carried home-made weapons tucked in our belts. A good shot was a pot shot, rabbit stew, pigeon pie. We knew our birds' eggs, carried our glass bottles back to the shop, ironed brown paper bags to wrap up our apples, played our games with common weeds, found our sweets in peapods and chewing gum in wheatears. We knew our apples like a fence knows a pearl. Parents fond of proverbs and pies were grateful for our scrumping prowess. Childhoods financed by the hedgerow fund, children built out of scrap. Our fishing tackle likewise. Whatever it was, if we didn't have it we made it, swapped it, scrounged it or scrumped it, and stabbed no one in the process.

We were, nonetheless, still dependent on the products of civilisation. There was one essential book we consulted before any fishing trip: the Maidstone & District bus timetable, half an inch thick of it. In an era of one- or no-car families, those buses were our freedom. Green and cream Leylands with wooden floors and thick cloth seats of public tartan, their numbers embedded in the village psyche: the number 5, Maidstone to Hastings via Staplehurst, Cranbrook, Hawkhurst, Robertsbridge and Battle; the number 84, Tunbridge Wells to Hastings via Wadhurst, Ticehurst, Hawkhurst and Bodiam. Hourly buses from 7 a.m. till 10 p.m. which ensured survival of the rural economy. Women could work. Girls could go to college. Boys could fish for tuppence.

The bus station was at the top of All Saints Road, next to Fowler's Field, where they held the village Flower Show, where the circuses and funfairs pitched up on the coarse yellow grass in summer. The bus station was a model of civic function and 1930s perfection. Shaped like a box of dates, long, brick-built with hexagonal ends, its feature was the glass canopy that ran like a hat rim, the whole way round. As the country depot, it had a drivers' canteen, work sheds, a booking office, waiting room and vending machines on the departures platform. Growing up began and ended here, on arrivals and departures.

Today the bus station is no more. Closed in 2006, for years it lay derelict, a ghost station where old pallets and broken glass littered the platforms, the last driver's note still pinned to the door. Tesco demolished it, replaced it with a Metro store and car park. Looking at it now, it's impossible to imagine the summer of 1968. Our fishing gear in a heap on the wooden benches, three scruffy squirts chipping the Fruit & Nut bars from the vending machine with scaling knives. Impossible to imagine, but easy to remember. If my ghost haunts anywhere in Hawkhurst, it haunts the bus station.

Kirby and Skinny are probably not the haunting kind, but should our ectoplasm be summoned for reunion, it will be as scruffy squirts. Knock twice on the timetable and we'll be there, two o'clock on an August afternoon. Our conversation might seem unrefined, but our fishing would have made your hair stand on end:

'Whatcha got vat bloomin gaff for, Kirby?'

'Poike.'

'There ain' no poike in Perch Pond.'

'There's pigs, though, Skinny.'

There's ghostly in the scene already. Our bus to Sandhurst is late. The Maidstone bus pulls away from departures with nobody aboard. Kirby pokes at it in motion with his gaff. We lick our chocolate knives in the heat, under that glass roof. In the cool shade of the ticket office, Miss Miles dunks a digestive in her tea. On the main road, the Horn's

Laundry van drives by. Behind it, Bob Luck's cider lorry. On the front it says *Here's Luck*. On the back *There Goes Luck*.

We push open the waiting room door. Yardley lavender sucked out in the stifling air. The brass pendulum clunks, another solid summer minute off the timetable of our life. Kirby walks round the glass case in the middle of the painted concrete floor.

'There's anuvver match fell off,' he says.

Inside the glass tomb is a scale model of the bus station made of matchsticks. There's something forlorn in all the trapped beauty. I can stare at it for half an hour. I grudgingly admire it, even wonder where it leads, why you do it. Mac has kept a ship in a square bottle from his seagoing days. It's on the dresser in my bedroom. I assemble Airfix kits and take part in the same deception. But Kirby, he's a poltergeist trying to shake the case, dislodge another match. You don't have to be in sympathy with the boys you fish among. Nothing is ever arranged with anyone specific. If you set off somewhere with your rod, you're like the ice-cream van tune. Your message, which might be *I love to go a wandering* means only *come fish with me*. Boys run home to get their rods, then run back out and join you, like iron filings on a magnet. Kirby lives opposite, Skinny two doors up. We're all hand in glove, at each others' back doors, smelling each others' kitchens. We smell of them ourselves. Kirby at number twenty-four smells of piss and rotten egg. Skinny Gould at forty-five stinks of his old man's chip shop and cat food. At fifty-one, I probably exude Swarfega and Vim.

Back on the platform, Skinny lifts his bait-box lid. His worms are a hot gas and look like burnt matches. A man appears from the toilets. He winks and twitches his head sideways.

'All right, boys? Where you off to then? Fishing?'

We call it Perch Pond. On the map it's something else, or nothing at all.

'Want me to run you down there? I've got half an hour, save waiting for the bus, eh? Save thruppence, eh?'

He wears a yellow tie with fox heads, half a drainpipe suit and shirt sleeves with elasticated metal armbands. His car is over by the dead buses, a kidney-coloured Austin Standard. Kirby has to stick his gaff out the window. Skinny sits on a cardboard box which crunches before the man can snatch it away.

'Lift yer bum. Yer bum!' he says. He puts the box in the boot and mutters something. Skinny had seen inside the box. Ladies' wigwams.

We can tell he's never had fishing stuff in his car before. We all know how to get rods and landing net poles in and out of tight spaces, what to bend and whip and pull. He flaps about, afraid we'll ladder his roof lining. He says we stink to high heaven. My keep net is pungy with yesterday's roach and Skinny is picking chocolate and dried worm out of his fingernails and chewing it. All the windows are down. He makes Kirby sit in the front.

'I'm John,' the man says as we pull away.

It might have been John, his name. He probably was a ladies' wigwam salesman. In those days, there was always a hot afternoon and a man who said: 'Hello boys, what you up to?' Everyone you saw said *Going fishin'?* Kirby said John was fruity with his fingers, but me and Skinny wouldn't have noticed. We'd found a girdle wrapped in tissue paper and tuppence on the floor. I can see why he put Kirby up front. The poorest was the prettiest, with his gypsy look from a gypsy dad long gone. Olive skin, big eyelashes, red lips. The red lips was ice-pole dye. The olive skin mostly dirt and grease.

John bumped down the farm track, his kindness reduced to a thin trickle. This was a trunk roads only car. When he saw the pigs in the field he let us go, reversing all the way back out into his own cloud of dust. We'll never know which of us he meant to murder, or if he'd planned to throw us all in Perch Pond.

Perch Pond was round as a hoop, tree-lined, a third of an acre, a gloomy, deep, dark pool in the middle of a field the other side of Sandhurst, the neighbouring village. After the half-mile walk down the Roman track, you came upon dusty fields full of lumbering sows, grey pink brown hogs with a taste for rasher of boy. They oinked and blundered over the indigestible stones and nettles, giant docks and corrugated dens. It was a short cut to the pond across pig-town, so we'd all split up and run, our weights and sundries rattling in their muffled tins, our already half-guzzled orange squash joggled into froth. When halfway across, thinking they weren't bothered, all laying belly-down, half oven-ready in the sun, they'd clumber after us like an avalanche of boulders. In those days, the journey to the ponds was always more memorable than the hours we spent beside them.

Our fishing on such ponds took place unwitnessed. Perhaps in other times it would've been a spectator sport, like a medieval tournament. The trees circling Perch Pond bore this out; like Christmas trees hung with multicoloured tackle, casting bouts sponsored by Pullen's. You could see who'd been there before you: Gibbon's wind-beater, Relf's Devon minnow, Pope's luminous tench float. The spoils of war. My own best floats were up there: quills, Avons, home-made self-cockers, favourite dumpy little perchers. Our mankiest weights were up there too, cast in hope of snagging a float back. Every spinner, plug and spoon from Gibbon's box dangled like wind chimes from the same branches. Branches which never snapped before your line did.

The perch weren't difficult to catch. We caught them as easy as trees. There were plenty of gaps to cast from, a good side-swipe had the float out where it didn't need to go. As long as it hit water, the pig-perch would scratch its fellows' eyes out to get to your worm first. Chased by a mob, your perch would tow the float like a caged rat bouncing off the wire, changing course till it had swallowed the hook and headed home to a tree root. The fishing might continue thus, a golden run, a handful of clean casts when your latest quarter-pounder swims past upside down however gently you put it back, then the next cast comes unstuck; no plop, just the muffled slut of hooked leaves. How easy it is, mid-dream, to forget those branches. You could expect a certain quota of luck, and this makes Russian roulette attractive for people who haven't grown up. Before your tackle had a decent chance to entwine itself for ever, it pinged off and was retrieved complete with worm, long since expired from the vapours.

Even as barbarians we broke for teatime. Morsels wrapped in greaseproof paper, a messed-up slice of apple pie, a flattened scone, a bled-through jam sandwich. Kirby had already landed one perch, a quarter-pounder, but, as we chigged on the grub, his swam past upside down as well. Our casts were like airborne viruses which left the ponds we fished littered with corpses.

Skinny was the accidental assassin. That day his first cast after tea was a bouncer. Everything had landed in the water except a tiny loop of line, a mere kink which caught on a burgeoning alder cone three feet above the water. Me and Kirby were settled back with our pipes made of thumbs and fists, floats jigging their way to glory. Only Skinny broke the mood:

'Cor, cor! 'Ere you lot, cor fuckin'ell, oh shit, oi've got one! Quick!'

Kirby said Skinny had hooked his own arse. Skinny's denials finally roused us. We had to admit, we saw the point of his wailing. The alder hadn't freed his line, and a perch had hooked itself on a pulley. When Skinny pulled, the perch rose vertically as far as the twig. When Skinny let the rod down the perch descended tail-first back into the water. We all had a go, the perch shooting up and down over the water fifty times, its blinkless eye accusing us each time it swung on its gallows. We kept insisting it wouldn't budge, but Skinny had long since panicked.

'Ged it off, ged it off.'

He grabbed the rod and started swishing at the whole tree, walking backwards and tightening up. I said he'd kill it. Kirby said he'd have the blinking tree over.

'Ha bloody ha,' Skinny said, 'oi godda get me float back an'oi? Me bruvver'll kill me. It's 'is last one an' 'e don't know I took it.'

Twangs rapidly ascended the scale. The further the line stretched, the more Skinny laughed. Me and Kirby took cover and crouched. The inevitable delayed no longer. The loud crack sounded more like the rod, but then you could hang clothes on Skinny's line it was that thick. The branch swung back into place and everything stilled again. The perch was swinging in the same place. We held our breath, the swinging slowed. Then plip.

'There 'e goos.' Skinny's eyes watered as he said it.

'Oh yeah,' Kirby said, 'wivout no lips. They're still 'angin' in the tree.'

We loved Perch Pond a little longer, but jilted it soon enough for other ponds where blind hope evolved into the beginnings of a plot for angling. Kirby's manky rod was soon a relic of last summer, but for every boy who wavered, another took his place. At the time there probably wasn't a boy in the whole village who didn't own a rod and reel. They were swapped and re-swapped. My old cane rod had gone for a rusty air gun. And the rusty air gun exchanged for Skinny's brother's float rod, which ended in the hands of Kirby's brother Desmond. The same is probably true of memory. You swap a nobbled recollection for a rusty ringing bell. Writing about childhood is to hold a séance, to eavesdrop on your own spirit as it drifts among old haunts. You see it through the wrong end of a telescope, then try to write it under a microscope. It's what you get when you see a derelict bus station and ask: *Is there anybody there?*

SIX

THE PONDS OF CHILDHOOD are simply those: the tiny ponds of childhood. Like school blazers, they're just things to grow out of in places of learning. I haven't seen any of these ponds since 1977. If they're not silted up or turned to stagnant green soup, my fear is that they've been filled in by property speculators and fly tippers or, worse, been developed into commercial fisheries with on-site burger bar, wooden huts beside fishing platforms where crack-heads fish for junk-food carp. Whatever has become of them, I've no wish to return and add them to the rest of the lost world. It would be like seeing the dead body of your own memory. These ponds were the sacred places, where you and your float became civilised companions, remember. But I must own up. There's one among those Victorian ponds where I might chance an evening were it offered, just to verify the past, though the fish were real enough. This was our school pond, in the fields of Swattenden. The best fishing days of your life.

The county rural, secondary modern school for boys is now condemned by historians of education as a blazer borstal, employment for post-war chalk-Hitlers and purple-faced colonels who drilled pupils devoid of academic ambition. The last of the rural moderns was closed in 1971 to make way for the plastic age already encountered, a comprehensive system for the inculcation of middle-managers, O level check-out girls for the new supermarkets or pen-pushers who drove brown cars up the A21.

Swattenden school still stands in its twenty-seven acres, a moderately austere, early-nineteenth-century grey mansion, ironic in its reincarnation as a Kent County Council environment and nature study centre. In 1967 it was a repository of the de-selected scrap, the eleven-plus failures. Few of us felt any bitterness on being sent there, for this was natural selection. We were the good bad boys from the villages after all, whose education was necessarily a curriculum of locality. No global village ambition, no equipping us for the wider *world* of work. We were educated along organic furrows, as if rural succession was a permaculture, not a threatened sociology. The object was realistic, community related: to sustain the life of the village as our elders knew it; to feed the farms and crafts which, in turn, had fed us. My fellow classmates were from families as Wealden as weatherboard: fruit growers, dairy, meat and hop farmers, stockmen, hop-pole turners, egg packers, foresters and tree surgeons, nurserymen, landscape gardeners, cricket-bat makers, tractor mechanics, growers, mowers and breeders, cider makers, saddle makers and gamekeepers.

School houses were aptly named: Brook, Dean, Hurst and Weald. The school badge on our blazers was the crested crane of the nearby medieval cloth mill village of Cranbrook. It was the luckiest stroke of my life, failing the eleven-plus. It kept me out of grammar-school town, confined within the landscapes I knew, among recognisable accents cut from thickets and hay meadows, not from the prep and band-box perfumes of the county set, or the conveyor belt to red-brick varsity. In fact, it kept us out of history altogether. Today, the rural county schools are all but forgotten, binned as failures, runts tied in a gunny sack, tossed long ago into a darker pool of rural reform and development.

The 1944 Education Act gave the rural head teachers complete control of the school curriculum. Secular instruction, as they called it, was a matter for the LEA and the schools themselves. The Minister of Education had no legal right to determine the content of our education. This left instruction at the mercy of local conditions, regional employers, preparation for a locality still known as *The Garden of England*. In 1960, the minister, Sir David Eccles, admitted that it wasn't his place to enter *the secret garden of the curriculum.*

And secret garden it was. We took our trugs to school and learned to mix all six John Innes Composts in the first year. Slackers were put to washing flower pots. And if you couldn't recite the Ericaceous Compost creed of 2 loam, 1 peat, 1 sand, you were sent to the school pigsties to weigh the wieners. Our gardening masters smoked pipes in the potting shed, had names like Mr Field, wore brown Bladen's on hot summer days and somehow, because we were teenage hoodlums too, organised us efficiently enough to grow food for our masters.

We gardened as we fished, but the food grew as we grew, less than elegantly. Even Mr Field's potatoes were the spoils of war. Furrows hoed, he'd trust us to fetch the wheelbarrows and trays of King Edwards ourselves. Paired up, gunner in the wheelbarrow with the grenades, tank driver pushing, we fought to the last tuber.

Mr Field called it Rural Science, but it was Smallholding for Boys, really. In post-war Ministry of Education huts all over the countryside, the Mr Fields of England attempted to address the needs of a declining rural economy. In context, or hindsight, it was a radical, meaningful attempt. Pig-rearing, horticulture, wine- and cheese-making, practical craft-work, hurdle- and besom-broom-making, haystack construction, tree planting, hedge-laying, garden-tool repair and maintenance, the art of the compost. It was both behind and ahead of its time, falling as it did at the doomsday cusp of English rural culture, the final days of peasant heritage. We boys too were subject to the denaturing of the times. Junk food, commuter incomers and industrialised farming were changing the landscape and the kitchen. The hop gardens were closing down as Guinness pulled out. The cider makers went into quick oblivion and the poor just stopped eating our fruit. At school-leaving we were sent to town, turned off the land, pointed wrong-wards into that plasticating final quarter of the twentieth century.

But in the moment, all we saw was school, and how to get through its weary days of isolation. Nature tested us. Under the rules of natural selection, the chalk-Hitlers and the playground pikeys between them practised survival of the fittest. In my first term, I was bound to the quadrangle fence with my tie and shoe-laces, trousers pulled down, pants filled with snow, put 'in the stocks' and pelted with mud and luncheon-meat sandwiches. In class, every master had his pet whip, cane, slipper and rubber hose, each with a name and a long oral history. Every boy with any spark had a protector, an older boy you fagged for. Mine was a bandy-legged full-back in the school First XI, Brian Tapp. Mouthy, hard, but at least not a candidate for reform school. I paid with my soul but he kept the animals at bay.

Our village ways soon coarsened until, by the third year, we were the bullheads of the human race. Take away the menace of the actual borstal boys among us, and I was one of them, down to the finest detail. It was the fishing which kept me on the right side of boredom and hoodlum.

The low point was probably when Mr Hopkins, the games master, locked us in the changing room, called us scum and said he wanted a fight. His hand in a running spike, he goaded us to hit him, then said he'd kill the first one man enough to dare.

The high point was fishing the school pond.

Secondary school had scattered our shoal of fisherboys from All Saints Road. There were fewer serious anglers than I would have imagined among the other nine-hundred. I soon learned from new classmates that every village in the catchment area had its pond, its myths and monsters. Each had its one hotspot swim where the grass was worn into hard dusty earth, where everyone had caught a tench.

By clerical inspiration, the school library took the *Angling Times*. Three of us gathered at it regularly, while others fought over *Motor Cycle News* and *Beat Instrumental* or a dirty novel called *Johnny on the Spot*: Chocs Redman, Steve Vowles and me. We soon called ourselves the PRV Specimen Group. Our brethrenship was supposed to be marked by the group rod and reel combo: a Sealey Octofloat 2, brass-ferruled twelve-foot hollow-glass float rod, and a Mitchell 324 spinning reel. In the event, it was only me who stuck to the rules come Christmas Day. Steve Vowles didn't need to compensate his angling self-esteem. He already owned the flashy tackle and we called him 'twinkle toes' because he fancied himself as a winger who never passed the ball. He lived in

Staplehurst, where with his angling dad he fished genuine waters like the River Beult and Marden Thorn reservoir.

The highlight of this alliance was our petition to old Rayner, the head, asking permission to fish the school pond in the dinner hour. The pond was out of bounds, round as a wheel and in the middle of the playing fields, between the under-thirteen football pitch and the hockey pitch. It was dark, weedless and tree lined, its bank a warren of roots. An old iron pond, most likely. No one knew if any fish swam in its rusty water. We had never seen any signs of life when retrieving footballs. For a long time it had gone unnoticed by the PRV, too unlike the paradise we conjured every dinnertime, the lily pads on dawn lakes near Tunbridge Wells, the June mist over castle moats, the chalk streams in spring.

We were in Popeye's class that year. When the subject arose, we nailed the mystery of the school pond's inhabitants on his door. Popeye was the science master, a Bunsen burner man who kept brass instruments under glass cases, and jars of chemicals under lock and key. Rumours came from nowhere, invented secretly and released like farts under the desk when needed. One rumour was that Popeye had dumped his old chemicals in the pond years ago and created monster fish who lurked on the bottom. The boys in DD's class, religious instruction, said Jesus had walked on the pond and performed a miracle. Mills's class, geography, said he'd made the pond himself when digging for artesian wells. In reality, it was a bomb crater made by Hitler with a Heinkel when he dropped one on the school caretaker for murdering his own daughter and always telling us to *Git orf the grass*. Most likely, though, we all finally agreed, it was made by Rayner, who flew Hurricanes in the Battle of Britain. He'd ditched his bullet-ridden kite on the very spot after bailing out and landing in the staff room.

Somehow, the wealth of our imagination, or our unexpected initiative, convinced Rayner to grant us permission to fish the mystery pond at dinnertimes, on condition we drew up a list of all boys suddenly expecting to convert into anglers. We allocated them a dinnertime by rota, three fishers at a time. Of course the PRV took first slot, credibility at stake. An invigilating master threatened a visit, to check it wasn't a sneaky ruse or vandal's charter.

The whole day was an unprecedented thrill. That privileged strangeness of getting on the school bus with my rod holdall. At the bus stop outside the Victoria Hall, I was the jammy dodger of all time, my actual rod holdall mercifully escaping comment. It looked more like a wind-sock run up on Don's sewing machine. Made of white war canvas, it had come folded in an A4 envelope through the post. The advert in the *Angler's Mail* had simply said *Rod Holdalls, 5ft with umbrella pocket, send Postal Order for £1.50 to PO Box ha-ha-ha.*

We got to see each other's gear for the first time, like that moment in the school shower when puberty strikes and the gaze becomes a shy or knowing one. I had no shame or shyness with my nine-foot Milbro Caledonian. It was a leger rod, half cane with a hollow-glass tip section, but I planned to float fish with a square-topped quill and bread flake on the hook. Vowles had no shame either with his big keep net and twelve-foot green-glass float rod. Chocs Redman, the third-year hero, the tallest boy in the class, the procurer of all our dirty books, the boy who dragged us all out of innocence by bringing one of his mother's jam-rags into class, the one who put bangers through Cranbrook School masters' letterboxes, well, he was the one with sea-rod eyes taped on to a manky doodle-dandy tank aerial. He didn't have a landing net or more than ten yards of line either. From then on his membership of the PRV was always in doubt.

At midday, we skipped dinner in the canteen and rushed across the field in our ties and blazers. We only had one hour and fifteen minutes, minus swim picking, tackling-up time, and all the rest of it. Never before had I cast in such haste. Any careless swipe to get that float on to the dark water. And dark it was, being early October, a grey day with leaves still blocking out the only light round the pond. I could hardly see Chocs on the opposite bank. Vowles was to my right, several trees away, equally invisible. They were instantly irrelevant because my float was plucked under in a greedy attack as soon as it fell in a heap upon the water. My shout of 'got one' was derided. The 1lb 1oz roach soon had them gasping and casting like clay pigeon machines. And what a pond it was, due, no doubt at all, to Popeye's chemicals. Roach-a-plenty, all pounders, all bigger than any roach we'd ever seen. My best weighed 1lb 9ozs. We all shared this scaled-up glory, this shock to lines which had seen better days, but never better fish. Of course, it couldn't last for ever, or even five minutes. Fishers of all ages make sure they ruin a good thing for the rest of us.

The list of boys on the rota was a traitor's hanging. Two dinnertimes of piscatorial vandalism and broken bounds and the headmaster banned fishing. As founders of this near miss, we were given one concession. Vowles and I were allowed to fish a Saturday morning in November. Chocs bowed out; a scrambler to mend, the hunt to beat for.

On the chosen day there was an under-thirteen football fixture on the nearest pitch, the goal just twenty yards from my swim. Swattenden were defending it. The ball kept landing in the water or thwacking the tree next to me. It made no difference to the roach, those faithful chemically sharpened pounders better weighed on the valency table than the Little Samson spring balance in my haversack. It was even-stevens in the fishing match before half-time. Our goalie kept shouting: 'Any more boites, Petley? Ow big this toime?' The two full-backs were relayed this information. The half-backs passed it on to the forwards. Then Holmewood School, the visitors, won a corner. The winger dallied behind my swim:

'Ere mate, is that true about them roach? They all freaks?'

'Yeah,' I said. 'They're all over a pound 'coz secret chemicals were tipped in by Popeye.'

I stopped fishing to watch. He was good, that winger, but he had one eye on my float and skewed his kick. The centre-forward said: 'Ah fuckin Aida, Bishop.'

'Keep it clean, laddie, or you're off,' Hopkins said. The running-spike murderer was referee and general killjoy that match.

I turned back to the fishing. No float. I struck into a different fish this time, a real thumper. The winger had seen it, so had our goalie.

'You got one, Petley?'

'Yeah,' I said, 'big 'un.'

'Bloody Nora, 'e as too,' the winger said.

'What's 'appening?' the full-back said.

'Petley's 'ooked a big 'un.'

'Ere, moosh,' the centre-forward said to the goalkeeper, 'kick it off for another corner, I wanna see this fish.'

'No,' the goalie said, 'you kick it off for a goal-kick.'

'OK, just tap it out the box, promise. I'll whack it in the pond.'

'Get on with it,' Hopkins shouted, blowing his whistle.

My fish was pounding about in tench-like hugs on the bottom. I milked it, making the rod bend, then over-loosening the clutch and winding to make it sound like a big fish taking line. The ball smacked into the water beside me. Twenty-two voices shouted *lost ball, sir* and a jostling of muddy studs came my way and crowded round the bank.

'Christ almighty,' Hopkins shouted.

'Petley's hooked a big 'un, sir.'

The thing about Hopkins was: he hated boys. He was that well-documented type of PE sadist all secondary moderns had to employ. Insecure, violent, isolated. Medicine-ball man. Ten-minutes-running-on-the-spot man. Road-run man. He lived across the football pitch, in the gatehouse lodge with his wife and baby. She was an ex-head girl from my sister's school Hopkins had made pregnant not long after she left. We hated him as much as he hated us, and I think he banked on it.

When we'd started fishing Popeye Pond, he said we were wasting our time. If he couldn't catch anything then neither could we. I'd seen his rods in the outhouse, behind his back door. Big drilled bullet leger rigs, both sections still up so he had to bend the pale-green solid-glass rods in backwards against the ceiling, like snares. I sensed the lack of pride, the anger that made him do it. We were jealous too. He could fish it any time he wanted, only he despised the pond and the depressive solitude of living within the compound of a school's echo.

He pushed his way through the footballers saying I'd only hooked the bottom to show off and to hurry up and break my line. But a fat tench rolled into my landing net and everyone but Hopkins cheered.

'Now get back on with the soccer, you bunch of pillocks,' he said.

The tench weighed 2lbs 12ozs.

A couple of years later I'm hitch-hiking down the A21. Fishing is a thing of the past. I'm at college and have a girlfriend now. A car pulls up, I get in. Bloke says: *Petley.*

It was Hopkins. He said he'd given up teaching. He confessed his dislike of boys, an emotional deflation for us both. He apologised for his harshness but, looking back, it seemed justified. A hard man who'd cracked. We'd already sent our history master to the labour exchange. He ended up cleaning the buses in the Hawkhurst station sheds. Hopkins said he'd calmed his mind, stopped drinking, but now it was me who felt brutal, and turbulent and out of place. I had the running spike, like it was the baton in some power relay. His abreaction fell on deaf ears. I just wanted to get from A to Z and he was only the bastard giving me a lift. The sadistic bastard who'd once pulled my hair and twisted my face into the ground just for lobbing a snowball at the Fuggles coach to Benenden. The bastard of games who'd said: 'What do you want to do, football, rugby or road run?' If I said football, he'd say: 'Right, Petley, you're doing rugby and Burgess here will make sure you get your face rubbed in the mud, understand?'

'Still go fishing?' he said.

'No,' I said.

'Pity,' he said. 'I've just taken it up. Remember that tench you caught during a football match? I've never forgotten that.'

How many times are we never present for the really important moments of our own life? Some are like photographs we send away to be developed, delaying the joy of being alone at the real thing. Some avoid the mess of empathy, when empathy is not yet due. Others are like an open flower when the one drop of rain falls from the sky. If we can't tell which is which, it's because some of us are born to learn nothing from the one true lesson a teacher finally gives *us*, and us alone.

SEVEN

THERE WERE DOZENS OF self-help books for boys on sale in the 1960s. Some of them suggested, by implication, that a secondary modern education was supposed to equip us for levels of construction, invention and knocking things up enjoyed by our instructors. These were men who'd Improvised For Victory in World War Two. Many of them ended up parking their Morris Minors outside peacetime Nissan huts and drilling boys for CSE craftwork. Bevelling wonky paint scrapers, or the cross-eyed practice of Whitworth Standard $3/8^{th}$ threads up a steel rod.

The boys' annuals were no consolation, still bogged down in war. How to make a naval telescope from unexploded brass ordnance. All you needed was to borrow a lens-grinding kit off your uncle in the Admiralty. Working field telephones for the holidays, authentic submarines to astound your chums. The false uncles writing these articles were made redundant by Special Ops in '45. They peddled DIY fantasies at the school railings with the assumption that we too had learned the rudiments of engineering with micro-meters, slide rules and sextants, and that we all had sets of Whitworth in the toy cupboard. No more, it must be said, than Mac expected of me. He'd taken his childhood to war, of course. As soon as Don had cleared the breakfast table on a rainy January day, I was supposed to pester Mac to help me build that underwater radio-wave oscillator I'd seen in *Junior Boffin Comic*. *All right then, Dexter, we'll be all-round autodidacts.*

These books were at least correct in assuming our dads were dab-hands, crafty, garden-shed Alberts who kept and catalogued every size and type of hardware doobry in labelled jam-jars cunningly fixed in rows along the wall. Everything ship-shape, serviced and proofed. I practised the drill with gritted teeth: linseed oil on my cricket bat, dubbin on leather, Jeyes Fluid down the backdoor drain, a tin of 3-in-1 the best friend I'd ever need. While Mac was rebuilding his vintage cars on sheets of newspaper, my godfather Dennis Woodgate was modifying Airfix kits and digging up Heinkel bombers from East Sussex pastures. These were the kind of men who oversaw my pre-life training.

Luckily, some of us inherited that other wartime skill: escape. We who lived among the fields and streams, the farm ponds, iron ponds and sluggish rivers of the Weald. The antidote to young engineering was fishing, where any level of ingenuity or skill was acceptable. It was all home-made, all bodged and wonky. We weren't tracking Germans. We caught as many stunted roach on crude, impromptu gear as we would have with balanced grown-ups' gut and finery. We were content to go duffing for peacetime tench with an Intrepid Boyo, half a rod, ten yards of bedspring on a spool with a melted wart from a sun-through-magnifying-glass experiment. We were the true all-rounders who fished all round the place in ignorant bliss, for everything with the one kinked tank aerial or Milbro Caledonian. Sundries we found hanging in trees, cut from hedgerows or bent with pliers when Mac wasn't looking. Everything was fishing tackle: runner-bean canes, hop-twine, corks, gas-mask bags and Oxo tins, nuts and bolts, fuse-wire, lead flashing, staples, coat hangers, shopping trolleys, laundry bags. Any float would do, so we chiselled them from dowel rods or elder pith or plucked them off dead crows. Bait was bread or worms. Stale loaves begged from Baldock's the Baker's, worms from the compost or a few turns of a garden fork. Venue was stream or pond. This ever-ready world was mostly undisturbed by the presence or instruction of enthusiasts or zealots with a mission to make boys ingenious and to fish properly, in famous fisheries, with calibrated kit and methodical intelligence. That is, till *Mr Crabtree* came and ruined that version of childhood.

Suddenly discontent, we hankered for a better world with better tackle. We were hurt and hopelessly out-fished by this demobbed uncle with a mission, and the time on his hands to fulfil it. His fulfilment is our beleaguered angling history.

I have in front of me a first edition of *Mr Crabtree Goes Fishing,* found at a boot sale in 1992. Inscribed by the original owner, *Ralph Evans, Harrogate, May 2nd 1950.* It cost him five bob. This isn't the edition I received for Christmas 1967 when I was twelve. By then, Mr Crabtree was every angler's false uncle and was running into an expanded edition under the new *In All Waters* title. Mine had a sea fishing section added sometime after 1950. In fact, I remember everything about my own edition, so engraved on the soul did Crabtree become. This indelible quality challenges all traditional lifelong highlights of the mental archives: actual Sunday school teachers, Scout masters, maths masters, the old witch at number nine, Priestly the village murderer. Mr Crabtree was such a powerful influence on your self-esteem. He launched imagination and sowed discontent, pretty good for a conventional post-war countryman stuck in the Thirties. With hindsight, I can slot him in as half Doug Cavey, half Mac. Army & Navy if you like, even if the thinking men who actually changed post-war angling seem to have served in the RAF. To further the contradiction, Crabtree is responsible for more blank fishing days through correct procedure than if we'd stayed in the chuck-it-and-chance-it category.

For those unfamiliar with man or book, Mr Crabtree, as created by Bernard Venables, is to fishing what, say, Sherlock Holmes is to detection – more than fiction, bigger than their creator. In hat, pipe, suit and tie, he first appeared in the *Daily Mirror* in 1945, and in book form in 1949. Species by species, Crabtree instructs his son Peter in the art of fishing in all weathers. Sales figures were staggering, running into millions. Like many things in angling, the myths so distort truth they verge on lies. Crabtree and Venables have been peculiarly sanctified by anglers who are dangerously nostalgic.

This book, then, is so important as a childhood reference that I can feel absolutely no affinity with Ralph Evans's copy. It wasn't mine, so it reveals only an outline of the true relationship between boy, book and countryside. It's the only book from my childhood that settled, that wasn't rejected by maturity, even when I physically ceased to own a copy.

It really doesn't matter who Bernard Venables thought Mr Crabtree was, or what he intended him to accomplish. Or even who his real-life inspiration might be. We know where Conan Doyle found Sherlock Holmes, where Richmal Crompton found William, where W. E. Johns met Biggles, or how Simenon cloned Maigret. Yet they still transcend their fictional identities in that mass-produced, prolific and iconic way of Mr Crabtree. In the present case, it's our version that counts. We were the anglers who cast our pocket money into trees because of him. We were the disciples who went out and bought gaffs and gags and outmoded implements we would never use. The commercial traveller in fishing tackle who supplied Mr Pullen was only doing Crabtree's bidding. And, furthermore, some of us wasted years in his image. Crabtree mocked us, all four seasons, year by year. His way, we caught nothing for the logbook or the parsley sauce. There was absolutely no question ever of the glass case, the exclusive beats of the Hampshire Avon, or much in between.

Our problem was as much with Crabtree's son, Peter. Again, we're the ones who would have kicked Peter up the arse and nicked his spinners if we'd caught him fishing down our road. In fact, he was the kid who didn't need to fish down our road. He'd have stuck his tongue out fifty yards away and oiked us: *My dad takes me fishing on the Hampshire Avon, so there.* Much worse, we are the boys who would probably have crept up on Mr Crabtree himself and chucked in a brick as he squatted by his winter eddy. Which is all to the point: Mr Crabtree's unreality was too earthly. We believed *in* him. He exploited our innocence. His fish were in our rivers and our tackle was unworthy. I pestered and stole to come up to scratch. I fished in shame when it all fell short. Life under Crabtree, then, was doomed to emptiness as soon as we peeled back that cardboard cover and saw (Venables's italics) '*The* Fisherman in Winter'.

There were alternatives to Mr Crabtree, but they were just locums and supply-uncles, generic factotums. As kids we felt them as brands, not embodiments or books or character-forming tracts like Crabtree. I had several diversions from the pipe-dream: *Teach Yourself Coarse Fishing*, for instance, by Peter Stone. The difficulty here was its yellow cover. It was a *Teach Yourself* book. Even to a boy this placed him in a position of passive ignorance, receiving lessons, repressing natural enquiry. I'd seen *Teach Yourself Latin* at a jumble sale and my sister had *Teach Yourself Pitman's Shorthand*, so putting coarse fishing into the same yellow wrapper made it clinically problematic. Half its failure was the illustrations. Like Crabtree, but without the action, they put all hope beyond the boy: pike fishing at Blenheim; sunset in paradise for carp; a weir pool in Eden for chub; the Royalty Fishery for the rest. Never a muddy farm pool, a flowing village ditch, the haunts of common little fishers, his readers.

There was also the *Ladybird Book of Coarse Fishing*. Paintings, rather good in hindsight, but fishing with *Watch with Mother* puppets was our feeling at the time. These were books given by aunts and grannies who thought they'd found the perfect solution for a fishing boy. Once, I received the *Dumpy Book of Fishing*. This was better, but lacking atmosphere and colour, the book you got for the Sunday school attendance prize. And one birthday, when I'd actually asked for *The Observer's Book of Coarse Fishing*, Mac, who didn't know a fishing rod from a piston rod, of course, went and asked Doug Cavey to recommend something for the boy. The predictable result was T. C. Ivens's *Still Water Fly Fishing*. Apart from the advanced literacy required, where would I find still-water fly fishing on a shilling a week pocket money? Why and how would I even want to go still-water fly fishing if I couldn't go with Mr Cavey to Darwell or Risden? Which all goes to show that Crabtree had no readily available popular competition. At least not in the world of Hawkhurst. In Harrogate neither, I suspect.

The radical opening chapter of Mr Crabtree is a masterpiece of subversion. *Winter.* In those days you received the books in winter and did the fishing in summer. Even Mr Crabtree seems reluctant to leave his bleak-looking armchair for the swirling skies outside the window. Winter was when no one caught anything in Hawkhurst, but out we went, heaving bricks on to the ice, bashing for pike. We smashed our thermoses, soaked our bobble hats, but accomplished the task, modestly set within our capabilities. This was simply to take the new Christmas gear on a maiden outing. In fact, from page two, the Mr Crabtree book exposed the great deficit of our life. In conditions where no Hawkhurst fish would bite, Crabtree lands more handsome specimens in one bleak afternoon than all of us put together had caught in our entire lives. Man and boy, the Crabtrees pierced the skin, like a rusty hook point. It hurt, it was spooky, they were weird; we wanted them, but how could we believe?

The Crabtrees bore recognisable elements all the same, but they were neither real nor unreal, simply parallel. They fished in a parallel world, the familiars of a slipped era. Those watercolours were undoubtedly our own landscape. The villages across the fields, the same church spires; why, you could almost see our ditches or stagnant ponds. But where did these rivers and lakes come from? Of course, this is the paradise of wet dinnertimes. This is a world for the elect who fish Risden, superimposed on the foregrounds, our own grubby ponds extinguished.

If the place is counterfeit, then so is time. In the real January, our dads went back to work. At weekends, all the Peters in the village played with their Meccano sets. So who is Peter Crabtree? His very first word, on page 4, is *Rather*. Even holy Kevin and his magic fly rod would never have said *Rather*. The boy Peter is supposed to be a token boy, for our sakes, our representative in fishing heaven. Not an Everyboy who is somehow born tribulation free and displayed by his father as an example. *He* is supposed to identify with his readers, not the other way round. And this little golden-hooks, this pancake face, goes fishing in winter wearing a Burton's jacket, a Tootal tie and short trousers. Even our parents, who sent us to school with plastic bags on our feet when it snowed, would not have let us out winter fishing in shorts. Peter, then, was just not of our kind, us *Beano* and *Dandy* boys, simply *because* his dad took him fishing, and thus made it easy.

Mac never took me fishing. He took me to breakers' yards or the dark garages of furtive men who dug among their tea chests for a dynamo, dragged me to the dowager widows whose sons he wanted to impress, drove us all to hell on the London-to-Brighton vintage-car run, showed me manly ways at the Brands Hatch racetrack. Wherever we went, there was a Crabtree-looking lake or river nearby. All Mac had to do was drop me off on the way, pick me up on the way back. Just half an hour fishing, half a dozen casts, was all I asked. My pleading was always met with the same phrases: *Stop your belly-aching, lad, or you'll feel the back of my hand.* We needed a book which dealt with that.

You knew where you were with Mac, but Peter's dad was more puzzling. We identified grown-ups by defects. In fact, I didn't know a single other dad who took his Peter fishing either. Peters usually had dads who were watchmakers or tobacconists or laundry-van drivers, stooped skinny men with thick lenses and brown overalls. One Peter I knew was the draper's son who went to Skinners' Grammar in Tunbridge Wells. Don once took me into his father's shop up the High Street colonnade to buy my football kit for school. He was the double of Mr Smith, the creep from *Lost in Space*. Mr Crabhands wore a cravat and had a stiff middle polio finger on his left hand. It was all dead, rigid and cold and it touched you when he handed the brown paper bag across the counter and asked if you didn't need new underpants. But Venables's Crabtree was a familiar sight in my childhood. I even have a photograph of Mac looking just like him. Pipe, gabardine, Tootal tie, thorn-proof suit. The days when men went gardening and fishing in a tie and smoked a pipe in the doctor's waiting room.

Actual angling Crabtrees were non-existent in our sphere. The men we knew with pipes and thorn-proofs were Peter-less schoolmasters, doctors, AA men, vets, nurserymen. Grown-up coarse fishermen didn't share their enthusiasm with nippers. Down All Saints Road they were silent men with runny noses and roll-ups on the lip, henpecked husbands whose wives our Don tutted at. Men like Bill Smith, who made his dawn escapes on Sundays. If we were ever lucky enough to see him come and go, we were spellbound by the bags, baskets and buckets he loaded into the Austin A30 as he wiped his nose on the back of his sleeve. Jimmy Miller and Les Crouch, bawdy lorry chavs, beachcasters and buckets in the back of the Commer to catch the tides at Dungeness. Eddy on his Triumph, a swing-tip ace whose bream bags won him sweepstakes. These were the anglers we imitated. Duffle-coat and bobble-hat men, their proficiency went unwitnessed. They fished away, on the match venues of Wittersham, the lower Rother, the Royal Military Canal, Cooden and Pevensey beaches, venues as distant from us as adulthood itself. Our world was the scale of an ant, of course. These waters were, after all, less than thirty minutes by car. Just the sheer amount of tackle they dragged round prevented any resemblance with Mr Crabtree, the ultimate minimalist with his rod under his arm and his hands in his pockets, living within walking distance of prime, exclusive fishing.

Crabtree endures as an English artefact buried deep in our cultural archaeology. He succeeds as a constant reference because he swings both ways: he's upright/serious – he's a downright joke. He is tradition, soaked in flammable ethos, the butt of pastiche and parody. He takes his place smugly in a line of minor cultural heroes and pre-Crabtree incarnations: Tom Brown, Billy Bunter, the grown-ups in the William Brown books, Roy of the Rovers, Biggles, Bulldog Drummond, Sexton Blake, hosts of them, in fact, most of them footloose after demob. He feeds a post-war generation searching for a comfort world of nostalgic life-enhancing narrative. But did he actually do anything for our fishing? No, I honestly think not. In modern parlance, he was a bit of a quad; a well-intentioned invention for farmers which became a total nuisance in the countryside when ridden by knobs.

With the moral agenda of an instructor, Crabtree's effect was to emphasise failure by demonstrating his own brilliance on the young angler. It was all right, we were used to this at Swattenden. A whole platoon of Crabtrees lined up behind the headmaster every morning. Pipe-smoking, mint-sucking, moustache-licking bores ready at the drop of a school cap to butt in and say *No, you silly boy, like this*. From quadruple equations to throwing a javelin, we were treated to what, on closer inspection, was an average but useless skill, a party trick. Every master had his own little Wallis cast with which to smug-down silly boys. We were never fooled. We knew they were sad old duffers. We mimicked them as far as the cane cupboard, driving those weaker masters into other professions. We learned what was essential or applicable to our realities. And here perhaps is the core of the Crabtree project. We were meant to fail. It's character forming, it weeds out losers in an era when success was not a democracy. Crabtree was as much about helping us *give up* fishing as sticking with it. The ultimate careers officer. Images of his bended rod were what remained in moments of cold turkey.

Such a noble campaigner is bound only for disgrace. For all his dexterities and perfections, Crabtree is part of a laboured tradition. As the all-round amateur, he follows the book and quotes the old masters, clinging to the past on the verge of modernity. The Crabtrees have all the tackle and fishing water they need. There is no point in them advancing beyond 1950. They have time sown up, and they seem to have inhuman skills, uncanny knacks, the uncanniest of which was to mobilise an army of boys to go to their Pullen's and start casting their floats and drilled bullets into water. He was created to help us forget the war. His peacetime finger pointed and said *Your Countryside Needs You*.

Crabtree, in the end, was only as good and as privileged an angler as Mr Venables himself. Venables ended life virtually penniless, robbed of any royalties by the *Daily Mail*, auctioning off his priceless angling relics of the 1950s to pay the bills, fishing half blind, accompanied by a float-dog who told him when to strike. A Mr Average in his day, careful not to rock the boat and upset our fathers who had just spent five years in hell. Mac's rebuild of a Sunbeam Roadster was perfection, acknowledged by experts. Doug Cavey's game bags and flies were renowned. My godfather's Airfix kits were displayed in the Imperial War Museum every anniversary of the Battle of Britain. The fish Crabtree caught, whose weights were specified in the first edition, were deceptively modest. Rural angling club 2nd Best Specimens, 1950, which might have won him a 10/6d postal order.

Sadder still, by the time Crabtree reached us twelve-year-olds, his philosophy was being challenged to near extinction by synthetic materials, and by Dick Walker's cold-war hegemony, a post-war pioneering of modern, scientific, angling theory and practice. But Crabtree's philosophy was tough as leather, which is why it endured and is up and running again after the dismal industrial angling revolution of the 1980s created nought but profit, competition and conflict forever to come. Mr Venables knew the world he pictured was already lost between the wars, but he fobbed us off with it. It's why he stammered into the eventual incoherence of some rather absurd, neo-romantic writing on fishing in his later years. A man whose first published book was *Tanks: Their Place in Modern Warfare* didn't offer anachronism irresponsibly. But whether we accept it or not, we are the Crabtree generation and we remain cursed by it.

EIGHT

CHILDHOOD ENDS IN BREAKDOWN. Ceases, in a confused and crumpled mess. An invisible marriage of love, childhood is the perfect union with yourself and a pact with the universe. But when it's over, it's dead. Worse, it drags more failure with it than any period of adulthood. You have to live with the shame, the broken toys, the despised books, the lost friends, the shrinking clothes, objects which only serve to capture that awkward passage. Suddenly, lies matter. Suddenly, truth matters; and conflict wakes to ruin everything. Worst of all, you go down the pond with your old rod and stare at the water. All you see is brown boredom. It has nothing left to say. You're sixteen and the pond is over. The pond you knew like your bedroom wall. This pond is now as embarrassing as the felt-tip freaks round your bed, the ones you copied from bubble-gum cards when you were eleven. Nostalgia, for the moment, is a pit in hell. Fishing there takes back all it has given. The existential intervenes and you cast hope into nothingness.

That pond of childhood was at the bottom of All Saints Road, the default venue of our fishing world. Our council houses were built on the old Copt Hall estate, the mansion left standing till the mid-sixties, its remaining land annexed by a hundred and twenty brick boxes. The pond was Copt Hall's water feature, part of a Victorian sunken garden, the objective of a long stroll through the grounds, downhill under chestnuts and monkey puzzles. In our day it teemed with stunted roach, a few handfuls of tench averaging twelve ounces, and sticklebacks of various spine counts. There were moorhens we called moggies, and a scuffling of water voles we called water rats. We'd all hooked something from the Victorian menagerie, when it was rumoured the pond had alligators, giant turtles and wallabies stomping round it. We knew that pond better than we knew our own mothers.

I was four when it first came to my attention. My sister was twelve, free as a pigeon, till she came home in tears with blood-filled sandals. She'd been down the pond, running barefoot, and cut herself to ribbons on a broken bottle. A doctor's job, stitches, tetanus injections and warnings, to me expressly, about ponds. So the pond started life as a dangerous place, prohibited and vicious, out of bounds. Don's limits were strict, and when I was finally allowed beyond the front gate, aged seven, it was to roam only as far as old Ma Aids's house up, and the Murphy house down, the limits of Don's view from the upstairs windows.

Reclaiming the cane rod changed those parameters. It put a barrier between Mac, Don and me. By fishing, I prohibited them on a technicality, by means of their total lack of experience in the matter. Overnight, my world expanded from two hundred yards to village infinity. After baptism in Ockley Pool, All Saints Pond became the centre of this expansion.

When the council estate was built, the pond had been fenced in on one side, KEEP OUT signs nailed to the trees. The fence had sagged under pressure of incursion, till it buckled a foot above the ground in one place. Once through, you found yourself in a dark, steep-sided hollow. The pond itself was shaped in a figure of eight, the channel between the two halves not quite jumpable. A spit ran halfway down the middle. The swims and the perimeter paths were scuffed grassless to below tree-root level. A Chinese bridge had long gone, but the brick buttress was there, the wall of torture when we hooked a stickleback. You swung it like a ball and chain against the wall, and dashed its invisible brain out.

There was one swim only which produced the tench. You set the float at eight-feet deep, squeezed the bread paste like half a thrupenny bit on to a size 8 hook, then lobbed it to the exact same spot three feet from a fallen tree by half-past six of a summer's morning. The bite came at a quarter to seven, as the milk float rattled from house to house. First there were the pinhead bubbles, then a knock, a dip, a lift. The float lay flat and trembled, slewed to the left for about five feet and disappeared. Every time. You struck and shouted *GOT ONE* just in case Gibbon, the paperboy, was on his way past. You wouldn't see him. He'd be fifty yards away, behind the laurels and rhododendron bushes which lined the banks, shielding it from the view of both pavement and houses. You were lucky, and famous, if you landed a one-and-a-half-pounder.

Unless it was raining, there was no point casting out again. The rain always produced five tench. The one-and-a-half-pounder was followed in sliding scale by increments of four ounces down to an eight ouncer. Each tench was like a sunken treasure; pure and hand-made, they lived in palaces on the bottom. The roach were their ragged slaves, the undernourished hordes you had to catch the same way as you had to go to school. Tench fishing was life outside the daily round, the things to come, the promise. They gave themselves rarely. They were the missing element of Mac's brief flirtation with the Bedgebury sunrise, the object itself. The folklore healing power of the tench wasn't exaggerated, but misunderstood. This 'doctor fish' healed inside, doctored the truth for a while, made time into a place. You left your blighted track behind, stepped aside into a moment reserved for those who sought it. Then, when all was done, at half-past nine you went home soaked, for breakfast. A cup of tea and a bacon sandwich, as good as anything you had in Bedgebury Forest.

Down All Saints Pond, nobody drowned, nobody fell in. We swarmed round it like wasps, to catch its swarms of roach, to boast and bull, push and shove ourselves up fishing's ladder. We both loved and despised the pond and its roach. We acted like we were worth more than this, that we had our secret Crabtree waters elsewhere and the pond was just the rules, the playground, that it was on the timetable of life. When alone there, we would sit patiently on our baskets and fish by the book, admiring ourselves and the shapes of our rod, the cut of our floats. In the midst of such sense, any one of a dozen regulars might arrive unexpectedly. Then we became public property, the rules were changed, there'd be a contest, rivalry, fighting. Soon we'd be tying leger weights on and seeing who could cast the furthest. If there were four of us we would bash the stickleback's brain against the wall. Around Guy Fawkes time, we stepped up the game to mimic life, not fishing. As soon as Pullen had his bangers in, we'd catch a roach, shove a lighted banger in its mouth, then let it swim away and blow up.

Who were these fisherboys who ought to be whipped? If you must know there was Gibbon and Skinny Gould, Tim Relf, Gary Reeves, Jonathan Thatcher, Slim Miller, Toad, Kirby, Smith, Weekes, Crouch, Peoples, Pope and one-eyed Jell, Kevin Spice, Phil Spice, Bones, Jones and Mansell, and all the bloody rest whose names escape me, their visitors and cousins and interlopers. All competence was there; all peculiarities and delinquencies. Hardly a boy down our road omitted to have at least one cast into that pond before moving on to tinkering with scramblers, skinhead ways or just going to work with their old man in a donkey jacket at fifteen. But in that inter-war period, before the war with yourself, between naivety and sideburns, you pitched your wits against the water, acted out your rivalries with the roach, tested lies on the tench.

We were nothing if we were not chancers. Hawkhurst, under our watch, was a village thankfully half stuck in its past. We roamed the grounds of demolished mansions, knocked on the cottage doors of genteel spinsters, were taught Sunday school by missionary explorers, all fearless women we failed to drive into other jobs, unlike our schoolmasters. It was a village where these strange and curious throwbacks to another age still dwelt, usually alone, with their lorgnettes and ear trumpets, tea-cosy cats and trailing roses over the door. Ma Butcher in Victorian widow's weeds, thick black coat dragging along the ground, wide hat and lace veil speckled in jet, a duck-head cane and shoes from 1880. Old Ma Aids, born in 1870, her garden nothing but rags tied round everything in sight, interchangeable with the rags she wore, layer upon layer, bonnets and shawls and nightcaps on her head. Miss Fleet, an angular flapper in crepe and silk and jet, walking through the village in tennis shoes with a fan and a pug. Nina Langley, our Sunday school teacher, the most fearless one of all. She who wrote books on Albert

Schweitzer, Antarctic exploration and a missionary memoir *Up the Amazon*. Green tweeds and brogues, her tongue constantly flicked out of alternate corners of her mouth, rather strangely, as there was nothing snake-like about her. Hawkhurst was an aviary of queer old birds. And it was, I'm pretty sure, the village where Richmal Crompton decided William Brown would live.

There is fair evidence for this, even if the author denied it and the speculation rages on. The most compelling being that the boy on whom William is based, Crompton's younger brother Jack Lamburn, who himself served in the RAF under the man on whom Biggles was based, *did* live in Hawkhurst. He moved there from Devon in 1952, hardly a coincidental choice, and was present throughout my entire childhood. The stories themselves are rich in the geography and populace of Hawkhurst. Thus it was incumbent upon us to do what William did. There but for the grace of William fished we.

William is a determined, natural, if elemental fisherboy himself, prone to inhabit the borders of truth and fiction, crime and punishment. Angling in literature is often a cover for crime. Some authors present angling activities as either embodiments of deception, or activities which lend themselves to deception, personality theft, or impersonation. In Richmal Crompton's portrayal of the fishing boy, even the title carries the theme: *William's Double Life*.

William, to merit this double life, invents a personality to protect the angler, the transgressor within. The story is a boy's classic: William, left to his own devices, decides to start an aquarium. He fishes the stream and catches nothing. He is in despair until he remembers the pond in the grounds of the Laburnums, a large house at the end of the village. It has a TO LET sign up, but for the moment there are no impediments to his crawling through a hole in the hedge, scrumping apples on his way down to the pond, where the fish, roach at a safe conjecture, impale themselves on his bent pin, throw themselves into his net and even willingly allow his hand to hoik them out. He sets a target of two hundred. Each trip yields around forty, and these he keeps in a pail at home. But then the house is let to a Miss Murgatroyd, a shrill neurotic dame with extravagant hair, a pious spinster with a vice-like grip, who loses no time in demonstrating her ferocity to the poacher. William is an uncouth thief who has stolen her fishes and apples. She ejects him and threatens to complain to his father. After lunch William is forced into his best clothes and groomed to a pomade sheen for the vicar's weekly tea party. *En route*, he bumps into Miss Murgatroyd. She is on her own way to complain to William's father. She suspects it's William, but hesitates, fatally, because she can't quite connect this gleaming boy with the ragged urchin who poached her fish. William seizes the opportunity to invent Algernon, William's alter ego, his fake angelic twin brother. Thus he pleads with her to spare his parents the shame, and promises to convert evil William to his own angelic demeanour. This duplicity continues, as does the poaching; two hundred roach are two hundred roach, after all, not one hundred and sixty. William disguises himself as Algernon after every trip, heading off Miss Murgatroyd until, as he himself says, *He felt that he'd rather let events take their course*. . . Duplicity exposed is a price worth paying for a big bag of roach.

I paid a similar price for a similar game, in Miss Murgatroyd's garden. There were three or four roach ponds in Hawkhurst's spinster gardens. They all had apple trees, rock gardens and roses. The eccentric old biddies who lived there with their pugs and ginger cats were retired twin-set headmistresses, or the flapper kind, often rumoured to be authors or moral versifiers. Knocking on their doors was best avoided. A disturbed Murgatroyd was not in a mood to let you fish her pond. Instead, you kept passing till you saw them in their garden with a trug and a ball of string. Then they might come smiling over to the gate. I managed to fish three spinster ponds. They all teemed with minuscule silver off-cuts which made the fishing dull unless, like William, you set yourself a target or involved some risk, like filching apples, strawberries and gooseberries. It always went wrong. No highly strung Murgatroyd really wants a scruffy boy hanging about the garden shooting sly glances at edibles between peculiar practices.

Theobald's, however, was a proper pond. This Murgatroyd lived in a modern commuter house on a private estate, NO THROUGH ROAD. Another splendid mansion built in the 1660s was demolished in 1961 to make way for these brick bunkers. The end two houses shared the pond. One bothered young trout refused permission, plainly not yet a Murgatroyd. Her neighbour, who may have been the mathematics mistress at the girls' public school, was all smiles and *Dear boy, of course you may fish.*

I own a postcard of that pond, early 1900s, a hand-coloured plate, wooden punt moored beneath an oak tree, a tiny bridge of ornate stick-work, blue water and reed beds evoking tench, pike and rudd. I found that postcard at a boot sale in Wales. Addressed to Miss Luck, St Leonards-on-Sea, the sender announces that she is visiting her *poor old aunt in the afternoon* but for the moment is *feeling better for the rest, due to being spoiled by breakfast in bed.* How it sets the scene: a Miss Murgatroyd postcard.

Murgatroyd ponds were best fished alone. But to Theobald's we went in twos. The pond accommodated chums and several changes of swim. The bridge had long gone, the reed beds were still there, and it remained a handsome pond, if treeless. Miss Murgatroyd was insistent we fished her plainer half and didn't disturb either her neighbour or the swan. Our fishing usually passed smoothly; the smiling Murgatroyd sometimes stood watching us from her garden, butterfly spectacles on a gold chain, white blouse and a bollard of hair over a puzzled, expect-the-worst expression. The lack of incident confused her rather than endeared us to her. Boredom set in after thirty roach. In fact, for such a good-looking pond, the fish were a disappointment. The teeming roach impaled themselves on our hooks preventing any other species which might be present from getting a look in. It wasn't the place to have casting races or to try out a new spinner. Perhaps she knew about the way boys fished and had set a trap to appease her own boredom in the summer holidays, having no Lillesden gels to thrash with her sarcasm.

Then one day Skinny came along. He hooked a roach, swung it in, and couldn't get the hook out. A minute with the disgorger failed to dislodge the hook from its gullet. The swan was naturally curious. It received few visits and had no mate. It drifted towards us and turned amidships. Skinny decided his roach needed refreshing before further surgery and swung it back towards the water. He hadn't noticed the swan in our berth. The roach landed on the swan's back, slipping down between the folding wings into a downy crevice. The swan, sensing an unfriendly act, drifted away. Skinny froze into the statue of a boy in the last minute of his life. His rod began to stretch. *Let some line out,* I said. Instead, he took the desperate measure, the one the Murgatroyd had warned us about. Skinny struck with the rod, hoping the roach would fly out. The line caught around a wing bone. The swan, irked now, turned and faced us in a huff. A shrill, neurotic screech from the Murgatroyd's garden look-out meant the game was up. Her vice-like grip was on its way. Skinny was now officially playing a highly strung swan on his bended rod. The Murgatroyd ran indoors and fetched a broom. Skinny finally came to his senses and slackened off. I threw a slice of bread on to the water. The swan addled back and faced us, sipped the bread, found it was good. With the angle changed, the roach whipped off. A broom appeared. Skinny cut the line, the roach swam home. We were last seen retreating over the fields behind us, pursued by a Murgatroyd with a broom, shouting: *I know who your fathers are.*

We always ended up back at All Saints Pond, the place of no ideas, the pond of lost causes. It was only fitting that childhood actually ended here and a greater menace to the soul than fishing was let loose. One summer afternoon, I went round the Thatcher's house to find Jonathan. He always fancied fishing somewhere other than the pond, which his back garden overlooked from on high. When he did fish the pond, his dad had the habit of appearing there. An unwritten rule, mostly kept by tradition, forbade the grown-up entry. But Mr Thatcher was one of those smart-arse 'all right, lads?' types with hair slicked back and a yellow cardigan with Guinness buttons. Once, when Jonathan's float had gone under unexpectedly in a cloud of evening tench bubbles, Mr Thatcher wrestled the rod off his own son, struck and missed. His reason was obscure, but seemed based on his notion that only a man is equal to the fight of a tench.

'That was a big fish,' he said.

'How can you tell?' Jonathan asked.

Oh, Mr Thatcher could tell. The speed of the bite for one thing, and the amount of line it took.

'How big was it, then?'

'Two-and-a-half pounds,' he said.

None of us was impressed. Mr Thatcher was an engraver and watchmaker, never a fisherman. Mac despised him, but by then all Mac's efforts to breech the social divide had collapsed in bitter recognition of who he really was. A social climber as misanthropic as a caged rat. A failing insurance broker with an office in Rye, where some old soldier sat on a three-legged stool waiting for his chance to work the Gestetner. Mac always kept an unpaid dog-robber in his self-employments, unemployable dummies who filled the chair and made Mac feel like the boss while he picked at his blotter with its dead-man's cup rings, dreaming of the rich widow who might come up the creaking stairs to insure her pearls. These ghost factotums called him Mac in private, Mr Petley in public; old men who'd worked and grumbled through fifty all-weather years at the same gaff, lost an arm and missed both ruddy wars by a hair. Semi-illiterate, they marvelled at Mac's knowledge of third party, fire & theft, or his black-fingered way with motor cars.

For such a misanthrope, Mac was easily impressed and gullible. Anyone who didn't live in a council house was a potential ticket to better things, opportunity, respect for his talents. He wasn't averse to using me. In football matters I was his representative, so when Brian Powney phoned to say he was coming to the office to insure his vending-machine business, I was bundled into the Austin and driven to Rye. Powney was a goalkeeper with Third Division Brighton & Hove Albion. I played inside-left for the school under-fourteens, up for a county trial, on loan to the Rye United sub's bench in the Sussex Sunday League. I was too puny a teen to push through to potential, but I was kept on as a goal poacher and penalty ace for the dying minutes, when I could run around like a whirlwind and look good against eleven half-dead coalmen. But Powney was an unlikely looking keeper, half-pint and lingering in the reserves himself. He wouldn't come out for some penalty practice over the playing fields, but Mac persuaded him to do a penalty prize turn at the Hawkhurst village fête.

Powney had a liking for the shows. Three shots for a tanner. He must have been in the beer tent before putting on the gloves, for in the yellow grass of a hot July afternoon, I put all three into the corners, top and bottom, twice sending him the wrong way. There was something flattering but sad about the way he threw the gloves off and went back into the tent. Nothing came of our hopes with Powney. The insurance flopped. Ends never met. It was all downhill and going short. Don was as bitter as Mac, and it was always a toss up which one of them would say *I'm sick to the back teeth of it, I am* over tea.

Then one morning we all drove to Rye with our belongings and valuables jugged and boxed and wrapped in newspaper. Mac parked outside an antiques shop and went in alone. Don sat crying in the car. Most of our stuff had come from the closed-down mansions after the war when the contents went to auction. Local junk dealers got the bric-a-brac leftovers the dealers didn't want. In those days this meant anything after 1850, furniture and knick-knacks. When Mac and Don had needed furniture in 1950, they'd paid Mr Connolly a tenner and he'd furnished every room complete, knick-knacks, pictures and all, as a job lot from the mansions. Now it was all gone; another 'friend' of Mac's had robbed us. All those objects I'd considered organic family attachments, the relics of childhood's museum: old brass, silver spoons, three watercolours of racehorses, 1790, a little servant's bell from India, two Swiss army dolls, lampshades from eighteenth-century parchment wills, a ship's tobacco jar, all Mac's war souvenirs, strange medals and weird coins from World War One, six thousand matchbox labels of the world, a Victorian brass fishing reel, a leather book from 1705, a sword, the cannon-ball, my Egyptian penny, an everlasting brass calendar. All the vases, tea trays, bone china, salad dishes, fruit bowls, kettle, drinking glasses, the tin I kept my brass tacks in, a tooth my sister dug up in the garden, and my clockwork tin car Mac said had come from America, an off-white 1930s saloon with a rubber wheel on the bottom which stopped it falling over the table edge. So as childhood was ending, they sold it anyway.

The paint peeled off the walls and the money went on coal and rent. The only furniture left in the kitchen was a fold-up ironing board. Mac found a job in Hawkhurst, spares man at the Esso garage. He became the only Tory voter down All Saints Road, delivering election leaflets, delivering incoherent moans about Harold Wilson every teatime till he slogged up to the British Legion where he had a second job as barman.

Dennis Thatcher was a social climber too, so Mac courted him shamelessly after rumours that Dennis's spinster aunt owned her own dwelling, a modest cottage with an orchard and an acre of paddock in Denton, a village near Canterbury. One night Mac came home after standing Dennis a Mackeson up the Legion, rubbing his hands with the news. It was true, the aunt was dying and the Thatchers would inherit and move to Denton on her death rattle. It solved the mystery of where the Thatchers went every Sunday. It uncorked the scorn and jealousy Don and I had grown so used to. Mr Thatcher might have been a *blinkin' idiot*, his wife a *gormless ape*, the three children *daft whippersnappers*, but Mac's humiliation threshold was inhuman. Come Sunday afternoon, we were on our way to Denton in the motor. Mac convinced us that somehow we'd be sharing in the Thatchers' luck. Don knew better. Our Sunday drives had always been journeys toward bitter truths. Don and I arrived, every time, but somehow Mac remained in transit. A summons to a dower house with his tool bag became an invitation to tea with the widowed mother of some vintage car crony with a collection of old rollers on the tennis court. Tea was me and Don told to wait in the car, the widow handing the cups through the window saying *Mac won't be long, he's just changing the washers*. On the way to Denton, Mac's bonhomie was unconvincing. We knew the ropes; they hanged us every time. Don's questions were pushed aside. It was a long drive in the heat, and soon all three of us were reduced to grumpy silence. A mile from Denton we came to a roundabout. Instead of following the sign on to Denton, Mac drove all the way round then pulled on to the verge facing back the way we'd come. *They'll be here soon*, he said. Ten minutes later the Thatchers' maroon Vauxhall Victor crossed the roundabout and passed us by. Dennis hooted, the kids waved. Mac started up and we followed them, all the way back home to All Saints Road. Mac said, *That was good. We'll have to do it again next Sunday.* And we did, half a dozen times. Perhaps Mac hoped Dennis would eventually give in and feel sorry for us. That one Sunday he'd say,

Oh all right, you've come this far so you might as well see the house. Perhaps Mac thought that if he could just meet the moneyed aunt and explain what a good man he was, she'd alter her will. Or did it just fuel his need, the righteous hatreds of the English, where even a puny watchmaker living in a council house can snub you to the core?

In the Thatchers' garden then, Jonathan's sister Elizabeth was messing about in a tent with her friend from next door, Bridget Godden. I was thirteen. So were they. I wore my hipsters and a wide plastic hipster belt, blue with a red stripe round the middle, the only thing I could afford from *The Carnaby Street Catalogue.* The girls were inside the tent. We pulled the guy ropes out and it collapsed. They chased us down the back garden. Somehow the tables turned, we chased them, over the fence and down the slope between the trees. Halfway down to the pond, I caught Elizabeth and we wrestled. We'd never noticed each other before, and never did again. During the tussle I fell on top of her. We were laughing. Something was pulling on my insides. She said:

'Get off, you dirty old man.'

I had no idea what she meant, but she was midwife to the serpent born, a reason to give up fishing, which was tugging me awake.

The chase petered out, the girls withdrew to reform their tent. I ran home, anxious to examine the cause of my upheaval. Don was up the shops so I stood in the kitchen beside the Ali-Baba linen basket and unzipped the hipsters. A thing I had never seen before emerged. It hadn't been there earlier when I'd gone out to play, with fishing on my mind. In place of that old puckered spout, a brand new changeling, a hatched egg, rude and pointing, its tip a pike bung. I replayed the chase, the moment I fell on Elizabeth, the brief rub against her. The new arrival seemed to know all about that. He even remembered the electric tingling. I pulled the skirting back and for a moment saw the horror of my insides, like a tube of writhing maggots and sinews. It was all right, only years of not doing what Don had said I should do in the weekly hot tub: *Wash behind yer wick, boy.* Underpant fluff had blossomed into mature cotton cheese. Pulling it away was as great a moment as pulling up that trout from Ockley Pool. I had seen behind the future, and could have caught a chub on it.

Not long after, Mac drove me over to Flimwell in his latest undead motor, a 1936 Lanchester with wooden doors. In a field behind some sheds, on a sharp slope with a dirt track where he said some boys he knew rode scramblers, he allowed me to take the wheel in first gear. At three miles per hour, his fist managed all the actual steering and steadying. At the foot of the slope, he let me make the turn unaided. I stepped on it and swung. We stumbled and the engine let out a yelp like I'd run a dog over. A red light popped up on the dashboard. I'd unbalanced to port. Mac took evasive action and ordered me out, told me to walk up to the shed and wait there while he parked the car and had a word with Ken, the owner of the place. Half the shed was open barn. I pulled out a drawer in an old table and discovered treasure. Naturist magazines, *Health & Efficiency*. Misty nudes. I shoved one under the belt for later and flicked through the others, the new knob straight in the pocket. The leaky roof had crinkled the pictures but a wavy game of tennis was underway, mixed doubles in birthday suits, plastic triangles on the birds and a blur over the chaps.

'Put that back, my lad! I've a good mind to. . .'

But he didn't. His hand fell loose. We both knew my childhood was finished now. Was that why he'd put me in the driver's seat? To make a man of me? That part of me which had no past was gone. Now I had a past.

Till then I'd even had to share his bath. Saturday evenings he'd bang on the floor with the Loxene bottle to signal he'd washed his crown of thorns.

'Right, boy,' Don would say, 'git up them stairs and leave yer dirty pants out.'

I'd squeeze into one end. Mac would have his back against the taps, scouring himself with a flannel, vim and vigour like it was a job. His scummy water lapped my ribs. He was muscled from ships, still bronzed after thirty years of rain. He must have noticed my shiny red pike float at our next bath. The first whispers of hair like the beginnings of a fire gave my youth away. From then on, I bathed alone and thought of Elizabeth Thatcher. The aunt died, the Thatchers moved away, as they do in all unrequited love stories.

NINE

ON A MONDAY EVENING in the winter of 1970, I set off as usual to catch the 6.16 to Robertsbridge. I never got there. One by one the prototypes of your life grind to a halt. At fourteen you slip dangerously near to giving up fishing because at that age you want to try it out, this idea of giving something up, as if you have the power to make decisions.

Since aged eight I'd been a member of the Robertsbridge Aircraft Recognition Society. We gathered fortnightly in the Scout Hut, a wooden shed on pillars up a stair ladder, not far from the railway station. The society was founded by my godfather, Dennis Woodgate, for Royal Observer Corps men who couldn't let go, the ones who never flew, the sharp-eyed men of East Sussex with evocative names, Roy Christmas, Phillip Past, Dennis Woodgate, Arthur Ashdown, Mr Nines, Mr Lundie, Paul White, Ray Avann.

It was a curious induction, the deadly serious, peacetime recognition of enemy aircraft. It was a logical if unexpected step forward from assembling Airfix kits, a staple winter pastime on rainy days or school evenings before set bedtimes. Mike Pullen was in there again, as all village shopkeepers ought; matchmaker, the peddler of those flying machine kits. It was noticed, probably by Mac, that I had an eye for detail. I understood meticulous instructions and painted my kits in the recommended Humbrol colours. Camouflage, undersides, bombs, fuel tanks, wheels, even cockpit frames, pilots' faces and flying jackets. My godfather's models were already renowned throughout Britain's aircraft enthusiasts. He used the available kits as prototypes for modelling specific aircraft, either for their notoriety, interest or rarity. His were commissioned, displayed, bespoke. They entailed formidable and delicate modification. The accuracy and craft were uncanny. He kept them in a box room in suspended animation slotted within shoe boxes. Likewise he had a collection of birds' eggs, nesting in beds of cotton wool inside dozens more labelled shoe boxes. At Mac's intercession, I came to his notice as an aircrafter. In the winter of 1964, I was recruited as a spotter.

A spotter carried a logbook at all times. It was my duty to log and identify every flying machine I saw throughout the day: airliner, freighter, transporter, light aircraft, helicopter, military jet fighter, bomber, reconnaissance, trainer, monoplane, biplane; they were all there, criss-crossing the Kent skies. Sundry equipment consisted of 10x50 binoculars, the civil aviation aircraft register and an Air-Band SW radio to listen in to pilots and tower control. I was eight years old. Whoever the Royal Observer Corp's Mr Crabtree was, I had found mine in Uncle Dennis.

My logbook was the same mini Lion Brand Don used as her milk book. Here she noted and observed how many pints she'd ordered against the number received, from Monday till Monday, and how much she owed the milkman on Saturday mornings. My task was a more vital one: keeping an eye on the universe. *May 15th, 10.35 a.m., Caravelle SE2, Air France, flying SW. 12.01, VC-10, BOAC, NE. 12.14, Trident, BEA, SE. 12.15, Cessna 172, W.* On Monday nights, behind closed doors, the minutes of the last meeting were discussed before we *confirmed* our sightings. Taking turns, we read aloud from our logbooks, sighting by sighting. The others checked them off. My Air France Caravelle would be spotted three minutes later by any of the men in Robertsbridge, depending on their employment. Dennis Woodgate was an outdoor man who would have to do his spotting over the din of his cows or on a tractor. At the cricket-bat makers, the others were indoors and could only rush outside intermittently. I was at school, of course, where there were ways to spot planes during school hours. I spent many a lesson looking out of the window. And once, in a primary school cricket match, I was batting as Captain of the first XI. This only meant I called the toss and hogged the bowling. At the crease, I stopped a bowler mid run-up to note down what appeared to be a Meat Box (Meteor) travelling at fifty-thousand feet in a westerly direction.

For each confirmed sighting, a point was awarded. At the end of the year Dennis added up the points. The spotter with the highest number won a prize, a flight, either in a Dragon Rapide at Biggin Hill or a spin over home in a Tiger Moth piloted by a Mick Reid, a mad egg farmer in Stonegate.

Competition was at the core of observation. After the log-book confirmations, we had the recognition slides. These were the All-England standards, the training ground of the true observer. Transparencies of minuscule silhouettes, flying aircraft of the world, flashed on the screen at various shades of a second. A fifth, eighth, tenth or blink of an eye. A Soviet MiG-17, American Lockheed CL-475, German Fokker Friendship, French Super Mystère. Pinheads on our retinas, Beechcraft Bonanza, Nimrod, Lightning, Argosy, Bird Dog, Silver Star, Mentor. More evocative names, words with metal shapes, the moving stars of the sky. Sometimes Dennis spliced a sequence of Super 8 clips in colour of passing streaks at unusual angles; again, each clip came in at under a second. Best of twenty, we bit our pens and stared in a trance of recognition. It sounds mystical, perhaps it was, the study of flying scripture, seeing in languages, crosses in the sky. We marked each other's answers, carried out the collection, held a raffle where the winner took the kitty. By then, it was time for the bus home.

It wasn't all indoor fellowship. One grey Sunday afternoon in the summer of 1965, we all gathered outside Mick Reid's old barn for our newly inaugurated annual flight in his 1940 De Havilland Tiger Moth, a biplane with two open cockpits. Uncle Dennis presented Mick with a pair of home-made wooden chocks. Painted blue, with pull-away chains and the registration number in red, G-AOZB. Mick cranked her over and said *Chocks away*, taxied out the barn, pointed my way and motioned at the second cockpit behind him. Another boy jumped in first, some tubby joker called Melvyn, son of a new member who seized his chance and bunked Melvyn up. I jumped on his lap and someone strapped us in under a criss-cross leather harness with adjustment holes and a brass tap-pin to hold us down. Mad Mick revved the crate up and pointed to the speaking tube. I put the headphones on as he shouted over the roar of the single prop Gypsy Major 1:

'You set?'

'Year,' I said, 'but no aerobatics.'

He laughed down the tube and taxied to the slope, bumping over tussocks, chickens ducking left and right like a water splash.

'Put your goggles on,' Mick shouted through the tube.

The field sloped towards a thick wind break of tall trees and brambled hedgerow. The string-bag cobbled towards it, picked up speed as the throttle opened, swaying and stubbing clods till the tail wheel lifted. Mick worked the flaps, seconds off a scrape and we bounced into the air, skimming the hedge between two trees with feet to spare on all sides. I recall no fear, only the exhilaration of an airborne ten-year-old in the grip of reckless danger. Banking left, our first circuit of the farm was a gentle fly-past, men waving from below, a fairground ride but just the poles missing. Then, without any flying about the bush, Mick climbed to four thousand feet, levelled out and took a run to clear the air, pulled the stick back, airspeed steady and up we went into a steep vertical climb. As Mick hit the top, nose over horizon, he shouted through the speaking tube into my headphones:

'Hold tight, going into a loop. Deep breath. . .'

We went over backwards, at 3.5g, hanging upside down, a few seconds of engine quiet, the wind flattening our cheeks, the foop-foop of the wooden prop, unable to expel the breath.

Beneath me, Melvyn was only held inside our open cockpit by my own arse pinning his to the seat. Inverted, the harness belts cut tight into my shoulders and his full weight was pushing me out, straining every brass pin, bolt and lock. If he hadn't bent rigid into the shape of a seat I'm not sure he wouldn't have slipped out. None of this entered my mind at the time. It was playing out as the grand moment of my life, upside down at just under five thousand feet. All I could see were tiny, square brown fields in the wrong place. All I could hear was the rushing sky, wind in the wires, ears popping as my stomach lurched and the blood rushed to my head. We went into the loop with a slowness so gentle, like a feather slipping from a goose flying south, as light as dust off a moth's wing on a window. The wings of the Tiger Moth were made for air; canvas stretched on wood, only the leading edge slats of the upper wing were aluminium. This was the miracle of flight, the bumble bee, the magic carpet, Icarus over Sussex. The wing and the prayer. Then Mick let her tilt, full weight vertical once more, down and down until you could smell the ground coming up, till we screamed from a temporary madness, saved only by the throttle, the stick pulling back so hard the g-crushed bones of Melvyn fought back, his skeleton grafted to mine. We finished the loop below the horizon, a perfect circle like a smoke ring, climbing for more, plaiting cloud now, twisting air into rope, turbulence to lace, loop after loop until we seemed caught forever in a whirlwind, like dust in a vacuum cleaner, a Catherine wheel in the grey Sussex sky.

This was only the beginning of our hallucinated dog-fight. Instead of a sixth or seventh loop, by then I'd lost count; as we tipped the apex this time we were higher than before. Pointing the crate at the ground, Mick stalled the engine and put us into a spin. We went down like a top, like a sycamore seed. By now the boy beneath me was clutching my waist. I doubt he saw anything unless we were upside down. My fear of vomiting had long gone, but something mortal within me was waking to the notion of *get out while the going's good; live to tell the tale in the playground.* The fields below were a blur of revolution and I doubt Mick Reid even saw them. It's the view from inside a spin drier. Mick's eyes, I have to assume, were fixed firmly on the altimeter this time. I had the flying instruments in front of me too. The altimeter spun like a broken clock. The other instruments had no setting for this, for Mick looked ready to drill us into soil. At the last possible altitude, the engine returned, and the spin straightened. Stick back, we pulled out and set off skyward once more. He had to stop now. There was no room in our blood or our imaginations for more, even if he flew with perfect pitch, looped both ends in the same place and never harmed a fly. But no, Mick Reid was possessed by his Tiger Moth. He banked to starboard looking for sport. A train came along the valley, probably the London to Hastings express. We dropped behind it at tree height. For one appalling minute I expected him to land on its back, but he did worse. He flew its length and inverted over the locomotive. Thus, not fifty feet above it, we flew upside down in hell's parallel for a mile until a cutting forced to him to roll out, banking hard from the Rother Valley of death, a double victory roll for good measure. Only now did we head for home, coming down in the field to a row of anxious, pale faces standing by the barn chain-smoking their Kensitas.

My world was soon split in two. What swam below, what flew above. As watercraft was honed through intuition, my aircraft-recognition cells grew muscular with study. Dennis sent me home from meetings with essential texts: the *Royal Observer Corps Recognition Journals*, the series of Jane's *All the World's Aircraft*, the *Observer's* books of military and civil aircraft, and various spotter's almanacs. My scores improved fortnightly until, in 1968, aged twelve, I came twenty-eighth out of one hundred in the All-England Aircraft Recognition Final in Holborn Public Library, the youngest ever competitor. Our ace, Paul White, only came ninth, if I recall, and we took fifth place overall in the team placements. There were six of us, and these extraordinary men counted me as one among them.

In their company, I journeyed far and wide. On summer weekends there were the air shows: Biggin Hill, Coltishall, North Weald, Farnborough. I remember the acres of parked planes on baking concrete and yellow grass, my lunch tin with its cheese rolls, Bar Six and Golden Wonder Salt & Vinegar, the men with their Super 8s in leather cases and the knowing talk of pitot tubes and after-burn. I lost count of how many times I'd seen the Red Arrows in their Gnats, or the one Lancaster, the Stirling bombers and Mosquitos, the low-flying Vulcans and dancing Harriers. There's something hypnotically sobering about an aeroplane close up. It's unlike anything else for awe and deceit, more so than a fish out of water. A plane on the ground is strange calumny. To a small boy it's even more troubling, and exciting, because you can't know why. Usually seen underside from miles away, a plane is a wing and a prayer, the departing soul of a dead imagination. On the ground it's an alloy coffin, a sheet of rivets, a three wheeler prone under gravity, a sculpture which cannot express its other life.

Under red skies, the journeys home were long. For the first few miles we'd be accompanied by the air-show pilots flying their own way home, barnstorming and hedgehopping. The mood in the car was always that of men having witnessed what they live for. The car was Roy Christmas's six-seater Consul. In the front, three abreast on the patent-leather bench, there was Roy at the wheel, me in the middle, Dennis on the door. *Pick of the Pops* on the Home Service, Roy whistling along to 'Guantanamera', the talk a slow drift to silence. Dick and Paul in the back, their recollections, gnawing in deep Sussex burr, of old she-crates and the faults in the F111, an accident-prone American fighter. It wouldn't be long till mention of the other 'she' on the minds of thirty-five-year-old men, the silence probably Dennis minding the boy as the talk shifted. Once, coasting into All Saints Road from a day at Biggin Hill, Edna Cavey was walking down the pavement in her purple slacks, fully Platexed under a tight red roll neck. *Cor,* Dick said, *look at the 'ackers on that.*

So what did I learn of the world, in the company of such men? Probably nothing. My sights were set at all times on the childish. The child isn't there to make connections. What the men said failed to fascinate my expectations or awaken the future. My opinions were probably not solicited, except on safe generalities. And yet I grew up among them and, at their side, saw a thing nobody should ever see.

On the first trip to Paris, there were eight of us in a hired, blue E reg. Commer Dormobile with nine seats. It was 1965. None of the men spoke a word of French, only the wee-wee, sheet-on-the-bed jokes. We pulled in to a rural petrol station. At primary school, we'd tried minimal French off School Radio. I retained a few words: *maison, ou est la plume* and *chic alors.* Shoved out on to the forecourt, I came face to face with the pump girl. I asked Dennis what I should say. *Fill 'er up, girl,* he said. *Fill 'er up girl,* I said, and finally the ice was broken; I was one of them, seven men in a dormobile. We pushed on to Le Bourget and the Paris Air Show, and it was here, the afternoon of June 15, that we were watching a routine fly-past, an American Convair B-58 Hustler preparing to land. In front of me, just over the picket fence, an American Air Force fire crew were drinking Coke and laughing beside a red helicopter. The top end of the runway was a hundred yards off, running right to left. The Hustler was a supersonic bomber, delta wings with four great engine pods capable of twice the speed of sound. She came in straight in front of me, wheels down over the instrument beacons. Spectators clapped. It hit the last beacon before the runway stripes and bellied, bursting into a ball of flame. The fire crew scrambled in seconds and were gone. I saw the cockpit canopy fly off. The pilot stood, then fell inside his own coffin.

It was a week of pilots breaking rules. Flying over the crowd, or below mandatory height. Spectators were frightened. The local police chief said he'd arrest anyone flying under 300 feet. But the aerobatics teams swooped on us without a care. Then, in 1967, we were there once more. This time the French were airborne on the final day, the home team on their show-stopper, their top-flight aerobatic team, *Patrouille de France*, flying Fouga Magisters. Coloured smoke, tight formation, up for a starburst and they split away to invert and reform after huge loops ending low over the ground. In pairs passing bunk-bed, one on top of the other, the upper plane inverted. They were close enough to flinch. On the final bomb burst one of them came in too low, pointing at the crowd. You could see halfway down that she was too steep, too fast to pull out. The Magister pancaked in the field in front of the viewing platform. From where I stood, a ball of black smoke rose over the dumbstruck crowd. No good comes of seeing this once, let alone twice. Every night for forty years I dreamed of aircraft crashing. In the dreams, I'm watching a plane cross the sky, knowing, waiting for it to stall, plummet, end in a plume of black smoke. I won't fly any more; I haven't flown for over thirty years. Back then I flew bucket shop to Poland, Russia and east Africa. Aeroflot, Air India, Uganda Airlines, UNHCR, Kenya Airways, internal freighters, Hercules, 707s, private Cessnas, Islanders, Tupolovs. Most of these aircraft have since crashed or been blown out of the sky. Lost in the Rift Valley, crash-landed at Frankfurt, bomb over the Atlantic. The Hercules, two 707s, three of the Tupolovs, and even the Tiger Moth. G-AOZB ended life in a mid-air collision with a Piper PA-28. The pilot was flying it from the rear cockpit, climbing into the sun over Redhill. The air-traffic accident investigation report makes chilling reading. Both aircraft were flying directly towards each other for two minutes with no dead-ahead vision until impact at 1800 feet. Visibility was 20 kilometres. The Met Office aftercast reported only one okta of stratocumulus at 4000 feet. All on board were killed. The Piper came down in a school playing field, the Tiger Moth beside the M25. It was the dream I'd expected.

So that winter evening in 1970, I was on my way to catch the bus to Robertsbridge as usual when Mervyn Weller ran up the road behind me, flashing a packet of twenty menthols. I'd never smoked or been friends with him. No reason or incident had yet occurred for me to miss an Aircraft Recognition Society meeting. Merv was squeaking at me to go and have a fag with him in the dip instead.

Boredom had its puberty too. Village confederates were few on the ground at fourteen. Hawkhurst in winter was a dead village mist over the bus-station bogs after dark. New influences pulled old certainties from their sockets. Smashing greenhouse windows was a kind of purgatory, when you were always on the rebound from one mate to another. It's what we did, without malice or forethought beyond a lucky throw over the hedge in the dark. I'd even joined the library. Not for reading. Tuesday nights in winter it was open till seven. I took out big sledge-sized picture books on war and horses. On the way home I'd sit on the biggest one and slide down the wet concrete slope to the bottom. On a good frosty night I'd get as far as the dog shit under the streetlamp. Mervyn Weller was one of those phantom boys already there when your life went empty for ten seconds.

He was a replica of his old man, a bus driver for Maidstone & District. Up the bus sheds they called him Junior. He creamed his hair flat and waxed his suave little pencil moustache. I was once in Wally Nun's, the barber's, having a short back and sides, when he came in and asked for a packet of *usuals* in a squeaky cough. Mervyn was a leak of sperm from one of Junior's usuals, a growing version of his dad in rickets. Pale yellow skin, hair flat from Brylcreem genes.

The whole street called him a creep, weed, a tea leaf. He was born to thieve like a piglet suckles.

I'd already glimpsed his 'empire' over next door's fence. The Toads were worse off than us. Tony Rhoades was Merv's mate but he had a suspicious abundance of goods: airguns, footballs, sledges, and a real Lambretta scooter. Him and Merv ploughed the lawn up with it every Sunday. One afternoon Merv came over to the fence as I chipped a football over the clothes line. He said straight up that he'd paid for Toad's scooter himself. That, and everything else, with the lolly he'd pinched. It was why he couldn't keep any of it in his own garden. The Toads were thick, he said. They believed Toad paid for it out of his paper-round money.

Toad was a loser too. He always said he failed on purpose. He couldn't hold his jealousy like me. His moods fell to pieces. Up the field at football he invented the Toad Blast Off after accidently scoring a rocket-goal. They never worked again, but every time he had the ball he tried one out. He just defoliated distant trees, split our lips, whacked us in the goolies, caused arguments and lost balls in bramble thickets. He punctured one Wembley Winner after another. Even Merv deserted him without compunction. He did catch a two-and-a-half-pound brown trout down Foxhole Lane though.

I never made it to the Scout Hut that Monday. Instead, I smoked my first cigarette, a mentholated Consulate. We stood in the pit of rubble, all that was left of Copt Hall. Merv promised me the wicked world. I listened to the bus pull out. My days as an aircraft spotter were suddenly over, and I struggled to understand why. Gone was the routine and security of men and their rituals. In its place was an unproductive chaos, needing girls and fags. Having your first smoke covers all exits. It wasn't Merv. When you reach fifteen, transgression has no competitor. All your aeroplanes fall from the sky.

Perhaps the aeroplanes had seen it coming. Lately at the Scout Hut, I'd tainted the beauty of the service. In the back of the lawnmower and motorbike showroom opposite there was a large perforated board screwed to the wall. Fishing tackle hung from pegs in cellophane packets. In the half an hour to kill before meetings, I would stand before the board, rubbing two pennies together. The proprietor would be elsewhere, serving out front or in his workshop with a Honda 50 in pieces around him. I was a careful shoplifter. Never anything I didn't need, only one item at a time. A curved goose quill with a cork body and yellow tip. A packet of hooks. A snap tackle. A single coffin lead.

I would miss those moments too. For their stillness, the cold concrete floor, the darkness of winter pressing outside, the smell of rubber and petrol and metal, the stealth, like fishing itself, and the man who never wondered why every second Monday evening I stood staring, stock still before his little board of fishing tackle. Mervyn had all this on his conscience.

He said he had the cash for anything I wanted. I couldn't think of anything I wanted, not in all that confusion. But I puffed out smoke and felt the years go by as Merv described his criminal empire. This simply amounted to robbing Junior. Junior ran the family finances like it was Maidstone & District Buses, from a big black tin box in the master bedroom wardrobe. The way Merv described it, it was a box full of other boxes, magic casements, lids and slots all locked with mini brass keys. The main boxes were labelled: Weekly, Monthly, Annual. Merv had lost no time in juggling the system. Lately, however, he'd come round to facing some potential flaws in his strategy, which till then had simply been robbing Peter to pay Paul: start pilfering from the Annual fund because reckoning-day fell farthest off on the annuals. Being sly, he began with a division, the Holiday Fund. The Wellers went to Butlin's every year, and a small but mounting proportion of three incomes went into the holiday box. Mrs Weller worked up Horn's Laundry, and Merv's sister skivvied in a private asylum.

Merv's friendship market had already cost him dear. The holiday fund soon gave way. Being such a pop-eyed, peaky, pigeon-tit creep, his only use was lavishing pop, sweets, comics, Airfix and all boys' clobber on his enemies or anyone who frightened him. So many began smoking and yanking because of Merv's Consulates and his dad's *Parades*.

One afternoon we were up the field for a game of football, smoking a few fags in the interval. The field was the old tennis court in front of Copt Hall. A figure in blue sprang out of the bushes on a motorbike and said he was the new law in the village. Old PC Flower and his pedal bike had gone for scrap. Sergeant Wyman was the modern ton of bricks waiting to fall on us. It was only show, the song of straight and narrow, a new bobby flicking through the village mug shots face to face. But the menthols were stamped out and the rest handed over.

Merv saw himself in borstal now, Wyman's first case. Guilty in the light of that solid gabardine astride the first police Noddy-bike we'd ever seen, a big white Velocette with a Stuka siren and radio blip, saddlebags and searchlight. Sergeant Wyman had daughters. They were different, like Royal prisoners, permanent victims of the law but permanently protected by it too. We suffered their jibes like we did headmasters' sons, more permanent prisoners doing sums instead of watching telly. We knew the vicar's kid was on his knees singing hymns in the bedroom. The doctor's girl was always sick.

Wyman's house was strategically placed between two council estates, a house like ours, red brick and concrete porch. The only difference was the blue lamp which said POLICE over the front door. This relation to our house felt like a surveillance. I shunned Merv and his rising panic. Three Consulates and a Wagon Wheel did not constitute being in his pay. I even considered becoming a policeman. Once, with a ten-bob windfall, I'd gone down Pullen's and bought a Corgi police mini-van, even though I never played with cars. It was like a ritual, proof of having invited the law into my heart while at Sunday school. The blueness encapsulated an ambivalent oppression, a good but jealous blue. And now I fantasised about extracting a police apology for wrongful arrest with Merv. I wanted the law to pity me because we were poor and *the law* was unjust. I picked at these emotions till I prised out a thorn. I really wanted Wyman to bear all the sorrow of being on the edge of growing up. The police mini-van stayed in its box, a relic from the law's crucified corpse.

Then there are the things you already know, your ancestral knowledge. You've already been there so you don't need to go through it all again. But at fourteen you do, over and over until you get it wrong. I broke into Oakfield with Merv, one of Hawkhurst's mansions which escaped the wrecking ball. It was still complete, with pillared gates and a rhododendron jungle. The conker trees were medieval and yielded cannon-balls, so this had long put it on our seasonal map. Like all the old Hawkhurst mansions, it had something to make our pockets or imaginations bulge. The fate of mansions was to stand empty most of our childhood, waiting, till obliterated by creeper and wisteria. Henry Winchester, Lord Mayor of London, 1834–35, built Oakfield. He entertained the Duke of Wellington there. In 1914 it became a military hospital and sheltered wounded Belgians. According to experts, the house was only noted for its porch of fine coupled Ionic columns. There's a photograph: chaps with pipes and officers' tunics lean against the columns on their crutches. Others lounge at ease with bandaged heads on canvas field chairs under the tall drawing-room windows. A nurse smiles because it's summer, and the men are safe. The war memorials aren't built yet.

Even empty, Oakfield kept this atmosphere of lost summers and wounded soldiers passing through. Till it was driven away by the bulldozers, the councillors, the fat-fingered Tories. The rubble squires, room-at-the-toppers, selling off to the luxury hoteliers, the commuter homes, the wife-swappers. Our conker trees were felled, uprooted and burned. A road bulldozed through the grounds. Oakfield itself was left standing with a small back garden and a picket fence. By the pavement they built a big brick shed with a wooden cross. The varnished hardwood sign said ROMAN CATHOLIC CHURCH. There were hardly any Catholics in the village till then, just this houseful of grey-skirted Parker girls whose old man had left them for a barmaid or the bottle.

The split-level, double-garaged town houses for the new Catholics lapped the edges of the big house. We waited for its demolition. The windows rotted out, the wisteria was poisoned. Most of the rhododendrons were wrenched out by the hair. A wounded house stranded on an island of churned-up clay. Our interest in it declined. We weren't urbanogenic, and we weren't welcome down Oakfield's. It was opposite Theobald's and likewise a No Through Road. Oakfield snobs mowing their fenceless lawns shouted at us: *Get back down your own way.*

Then Merv said there was a builder's sign outside Oakfield. They were doing it up for Lord Snooty.

After dark in the dirty wet mist one February evening, me and Merv sneaked round the back of Oakfield. It was me who had to shin up the drainpipe and in through an open grille. I landed in the pantry toilet. A rusty key hanging on cobweb and string unclotted the backdoor lock after a few double twists. The wooden floorboards creaked under our shoes. I don't know what we expected. This was no cartoon. Merv looked for cash, of course. I went for the atmosphere. I wanted to feel how snobs possessed a place like this, which route your daily life had to follow in somewhere so huge. Perhaps I needed to know if I felt like Mac about life. But the smell of new pine and paint displaced any insight into that limbo between dereliction and renovation.

There was not a bent farthing in cash. There was nothing we needed. All we found was the debris of Fryer & Sons, the builders, and Chiesman & Son, plumbers. Then Merv kicked over a row of empty beer bottles. I trampled in his panic and a set of tools flew sideways. I collided with his flailing elbows, blundering into the unshuttered drawing room where a streetlamp zapped us bull's-eye. Merv's face was leper-yellow and he gawked through the big windows. I'd discovered what I came for, after all. Disappointment. I've felt it since, when seeing the privileged stripped of all poetic decoration. Underneath, their ordinariness is stifling.

I burgled a poxy torch, ratchet screwdriver and a two-bob penknife with just the bottle opener left. It fell through the rip in my old school-anorak pocket, into the lining. There was nothing else to detain us, just cold tea in a thermos cup on an upturned tea chest. Runt-brain was angry and smashed a beer bottle in the fireplace. I threw cold tea over new plasterboards.

It even felt like Swattenden on a Saturday morning, that empty house, when you went in for football and it was just a deserted mansion, probably built by the same bloke. Stripped of its nine hundred cowering boys, it lost its authority. You could smash its windows and scratch *Rayner is a cunt* on his door, but you didn't. It was like seeing a master on a Saturday, doing his shopping in his black A30, a seedy old bachelor who'd bought himself a Mars Bar to eat in front of the telly, on his own till Monday morning. A stabbing of embarrassed pain went through you, and even in your ignorance you felt sorry for this wanker you called Puffing Billy, the bloke who only taught the C stream cories about artesian wells when he'd never even seen one himself. Yeah, whatever I did, whatever I became, I'd have to do it for the likes of Puffing Billy too, and even Mac, why not? It wasn't their fault the Thatchers took it all and even burnt their leftovers, just so we wouldn't get our hands on whatever it was they thought they had.

Once outside, Merv pranced about like he'd won the pools, immune to detection. I was tiptoeing along the mossy border. Merv was bragging in the gravel drive. Giant tape measure big as a discus. G-cramp, plumb-line, light switch. Even the fucking salt-pot for old Chiesman's boiled egg. There was a noise like an owl or nightjar. Blip-blip. My ornithology wasn't as sharp as Merv's. His was the lightning reflex of a born coward. He knock-kneed himself invisible as I was swiped across the guts by Sergeant Wyman's searchlight. Like a streak of shite I was in the bushes too, dumping my pocket linings right down to the fluff.

'COME ON, SONNY JIM, SHOW YERSELF.'

I stepped into the beam, hearing a light switch and salt-pot clip through wet branches into leaf mould. Sergeant Wyman sat like a rhino on his bike.

'Now, laddie, where's yer mate?'

'What mate?'

I wasn't shielding him from the law, the runt. I was just ashamed to be found with him and sure he'd blame me. Wyman cupped his hands into a megaphone.

'LISTEN, LADDIE. IF YOU DONT LEAVE THEM BUSHES ON A COUNT OF TEN I'LL 'AVE YOUR GUTS F'GARTERS. 1. . . 2. . . 3. . .'

At 7 there was a rat scuffle in the bushes and Merv legged it across the gap towards the backyard thinking he could escape over the golf course. Wyman was off his noddy like a cannon-ball.

'STAND STILL, LADDIE, OR I SHOOT.'

Poor Merv, face like a plastic owl, really believed he had a gun. Sergeant Wyman turned to me with a sorry expression.

'Ooz zat, then, Scotch Mist?'

He let us off after a lecture, on account of our dads being 'decent fellas'. The remark struck me, but probably bounced off. Mac, a decent fella, somewhere, to someone. That should be enough, I should have understood, but I couldn't read in the dark.

Merv still followed me, thinking we were sharing a prison cell now. He kept up the pestering till we were soon back on the Consulates, dragging hard with cupped hands. He would brag as my head spun and smoke poured from my mouth like a Magister in peril. One moment Merv was a half-crown hurricane, the next our victim, robbed and beaten for his money. His threats to expose us all were becoming hysterical. Even Toad had started dumping his gains. I told Merv to just stop pinching and make Toad ditch the scooter. He said he couldn't. He was in too far, he had taken too much, and they would find out anyway. But once he'd dried his eyes, he lost no sleep over his predicament. He would start all over again at school next day, outside the Swattenden tuck shop when Chocs and Tufty got him by the ankles and shook him upside down. The silver cascaded out of him like amateur magic. He was trading again. Wagon Wheels, Jammy Dodgers, Cherry Vimto. *The Milky Bars are on me,* he'd shout.

Then he was gone. The Wellers moved very suddenly to Tunbridge Wells. Junior had jumped the buses and bought a corner shop. Even Don said *Queer, must have fiddled the insurance.* Relief at Mervyn's departure was short lived. Winds of change, they'd already stripped the trees, fouled the once-clear water. The school vocational tour marked the end of our educational passage. A coal mine and a zip factory in the Rhondda Valley. My first Double Diamond in Bristol, as we tipped litterbins over parked cars at midnight. The way school ends the world over.

The last time I fished All Saints Pond was as a post-decimal specimen hunter with nowhere to go except to circle in the dank eddy of youth. Some dignity was saved by eel fishing. Twenty-nine nights in a row to prove there were eels in All Saints Pond. Twenty-nine nights without a whisper. Retrospective haunting, a life condemned to walk the night. One night halfway at 2.30 a.m., two Alsatians came by. They were Don Ham's, the ex-boxer and stock-car racer, the All Saints hard. Hard of fist and drink. His Alsatians were ex-police dogs. They nosed out my cheese sandwiches, tearing through the paper bag. I backed off and they stood guard beside my rods. If I moved forward they snarled, then one of them lunged and I retreated out on to the road. They wouldn't leave, pacing around my swim like tigers in a zoo. I walked up to the bus station and down Water Lane to the police house. I didn't have the nerve to wake Sergeant Wyman up, so I dialled 999 from the callbox. The night copper said they wouldn't be coming out unless the Alsatians drew blood.

By night number thirty, I was unhinged from lack of sleep. But it rained. I was fishing three rods, a bunch of lobworms on size 2 Sealey Flashpoints, wire trace and link legers in the '70s style. I had five runs and landed all five fish. They were tench from a swim where tench were never caught. They were bigger than any tench known to be in there. Two-and-a-half to three-and-a-half pounds each. On huge hooks and wire that even as boys we would have shunned as crude. What a swindle childhood is. A pack of Mr Crabtree's lies.

TEN

MERCERS WAS A MODEST, private estate of twelve red-brick chalet-bungalows and coach houses. No fences, only rose borders and fake wells on a hump of lawn with the startling addition, to me, that was, of two-car garages with up and over blue metal doors. Some bungalows had fancy, local history names, some just numbers. Yet again a sign said NO THROUGH ROAD, which here meant bank managers with headaches, grammar school blazers on the hall stand, one swimming pool and twitching curtains. Mercers ended abruptly at a tall fir hedge, the other side of which was All Saints Road.

Mercers, like All Saints, had once been a mansion and grounds. The mansion had been called Highfields and was built by the historian Sir Richard Kilburn as a school in the mid-1600s. When demolished in 1967 it was an ex-girls' prep. I remember standing with Mac in a hole in the ground full of brick dust, plaster and batten. Beyond us, a sea of mud stretched as far as the first house of All Saints Road. Like the Rother floods, you went to sightsee demolished mansions.

Whatever the political will of the time, the destruction of historic buildings was like a revenge act by insecure councillors, often jumped-up squires with scores to settle. The usual petty corruption among building firms meant fortunes were made in the building trade between 1950 and 1970 in Hawkhurst. Everyone was on the fiddle. Social equality was the first victim. Minus its landed gentry, Hawkhurst merely stratified under expansion. Once the council began grabbing the land, the private developers did likewise. The village became ringed in by commuter estates for middle-class incomers, two-car garages, and that curious fenceless trend, like liberated households living without doors on the toilet. Thus Hawkhurst acquired wife-swapping parties, alcoholism, divorce, a psychiatric outpatients' clinic and anomie. In less than two decades, Hawkhurst changed from the quiet homogenous, Wealden village of the *William* books, to the brash, public amenity of a Tunbridge Wells-type overspill for the professionally anxious. It shoved the All Saints originals aside and encouraged the new money to take the village over. Their women drove French saloons half-drunk and shopped in town. The men drove company cruisers up to London and fell asleep at the wheel. Amateur dramatics flourished and a hideous, teetotal supermarket made of windows replaced an historic department store at the crossroads. The family shopkeepers fell like a house of cards and so did we. Today, a council house in All Saints Road sells for a third of a million pounds. Unlike our right-to-buy neighbours, Mac and Don rented theirs till death, and I'm proud of them for that. A Mercers bungalow sells for half a million. Contemporary Hawkhurst has a Budgens, a Tesco Metro Store, a digital cinema and a population which has almost trebled since my day. Hawkhurst greenfield sites are used as a dumping ground for housing quotas by Tunbridge Wells Borough Council. The deeply historic village of my childhood has become a gold rush frontier, a paved-over satellite town for traffic jams and litter louts. The demolition of historic buildings actually continues: 2015 saw the destruction of an edifice of mid-Victorian philanthropy, Dr Barnardo's Babies Castle.

One Sunday evening at the beginning of the summer holidays in 1971, I found myself walking through Mercers for the first time in my life. I was looking for *Almeida*, home of Sarah Jeffery, the hippiest snob in the village, the branch secretary of the School's Action Union. I'd been sent there by two student freaks with fertile names. They'd turned up at Swattenden one dinnertime in the final week of term. Nine hundred of us swarming the grounds, fifty-aside football, split-the-kipper, lounging under oak and elm. The girl Bryony handed out leaflets urging us to *Smash The Dictatorship of The Head*. I'd willingly sided with them in the inevitable stand-off; these two crushed velvet visionaries on a moped, coming into my life on a cloud of patchouli like distant lanterns on the edge of darkness. In the skirmish led by Hopkins and Colonel Campbell, I refused to hand my leaflets over, loyal to the 'long-haired yobs'. Rayner expelled me on the spot. I hadn't even said goodbye to my fellow anglers.

I knocked on the back door of *Almeida*, heart banging louder than my timid knuckle. Mrs Jeffery answered. I'd seen her about the village in her grey skirt and tight wiry hair. She was a substitute teacher who worked part-time in the library and drove a blue Triumph Herald. And yet she greeted me like it was the most natural thing in the world, me turning up on a Sunday evening when the church bells rang round the shire and you didn't call on your betters. In our house of a Sunday evening, Don did the ironing to *Sing Something Simple* and the world knew not to come a-calling. Not ever.

'Oh, hello there,' Mrs Jeffery said.

'Can I speak to Sarah, please?'

'SARAH! Someone to see you,' she shouted behind her, into the bungalow.

It was that easy. The guitar playing stopped. There were bare feet coming over the parquet floor. I could smell sausage rolls baking in the oven. A fat brown and white cat stuck its head round the corner. A half-open, sliding wooden door, books and potted plants in the lounge. A gentle, happy, peaceful house. Was this what Mac had been looking for all this time, only like me he'd confused it with the closed-shop of wealth and class?

Back in spring I'd chucked cow shit at this Jeffery girl. She'd been out walking in Little Switzerland, the local name for a valley at the bottom of the fields skirting All Saints, trailing her little brother behind her as she often did. You saw her everywhere, walking past the ponds we fished, paddling in the streams. Always barefoot, sometimes in a long, flower-print cotton dressing gown, her thick wiry hair held tight to her head by a fat embroidered band. Sometimes she had a velvet choker or a great looped string of wooden beads swinging on a tie-dyed granddad shirt which hung out over red flared jeans. Or this long, flowing green skirt which dragged along the ground and had thistles caught on the hem. I'd seen her alight from the school bus too. She was a TWIGGS, Tunbridge Wells Girls' Grammar School, where Virginia Wade had been head girl. Dark blue Sarah with her long navy socks always pulled right up inside the hem of her skirt. Apart from her brother, I'd never seen her with anyone else, which added to her weirdness, her aloof, unapproachable, unfathomable superiority. There had been rumours that they'd 'had to send her away once'. Me, Wayne and Reeves were over Little Switzerland that spring day, by the stagnant pond, wondering if there was anything in it worth fishing for. Reeves reckoned there were eels, but we only ever saw sticklebacks. Unless you climbed back up the hump, you couldn't see the field from the pond. Wayne peered back over for no real reason.

'Quick, 'ide,' he said. ''Ere comes that weird Jeffery girl.'

We waited till she was level with us then lobbed our cowpat grenades over the top.

'Stop it,' she said.

We peeped over, her brother was running away.

'Come back, Mark,' she said, 'it's only the good bad boys from the lonely farms.'

She was now a skiff of approaching bare feet, about to emerge from the corridor. It was too late to run away. She appeared in a calico smock and the red flares, her walk a bounce. Before she opened her mouth, I was in love and she was irreplaceable.

Close up, she was not the Crystal-Tipps you thought she was at a distance. Dry lips, thick eye-brows, straight nose, hair like wire wool, teeth like a breadknife. But her voice, her mind, her atmosphere were enthralling enough to transpose her into any vision you wanted. And she smelled of apples, not chips and hops.

Just one hour sitting on Sarah's back lawn of a summer's evening, and I drowned in the unknown, drowned willingly in the undreamed of, the unheard of, the words, just the new words, more than all the old words, which brought on a hunger. From Sarah's mouth, language was a song: *ego trip, schizophrenic, Freudian, bourgeois, Sibelius, symbolic,*

bestiary, Medieval, connotation, Marxist, Harrods, macrobiotic, rip-off,
Little Red Schoolbook, image, subconscious.

We ate supper on the back lawn, in the shade beside a rock garden.
I mean her parents let her. With Don and Mac it was tea at the table
with your mouth shut. You didn't upset Mac on a Sunday. You ate your
humble pie and took your medicine afterwards. They wouldn't have
let a single cheese rind from our larder go down a visitor's throat. But
Mrs Jeffery insisted I had some supper with Sarah; hot sausage rolls,
bread and cheddar, chutney, Shloer's apple juice. It was the first time
I'd ever drunk apple juice; curious, as Bob Luck's cider maker's was
only a few miles away and apples had always been a perk of childhood
in a village surrounded by orchard. You could only buy Shloer's up the
chemist's shop. Sitting cross-legged on the grass, the SAU was brushed
aside. Instead, Sarah asked me if I wrote poetry. The question seemed so
normal, the prompted feeling so convincing. All those years squandered
on fishing when I should have been writing poetry. I answered yes. The
profundity of that yes hit me. Once, a cane rod had changed my life.
Now I'd be a poet, because Sarah was a poet and had already changed
my life. Where the poems would come from I hadn't considered. There
were no poems under the work bench, in that Oxo tin. In the fourth
year, the school had produced a Gestetner magazine on green-and rose-
coloured A4, *Verse from the Den.* Petley of 4a had written one. I only
remember the lines:

The gallows were erected,
The sun went down,
A shadow of death
Fell over the town. . .

Sarah asked me if I'd heard of T. S. Eliot. She said she wanted to
write like him. His *Collected Poems* were fetched from her room. She
picked out random lines and held me spellbound in ignorance. Next
came Dylan Thomas and John Clare. Did I like Modigliani? Had I read
the *Thoughts of Chairman Mao*, or Karl Marx? Names which wiped
Mr Crabtree into the eddy of abandoned toys. Any brief notion of
introducing Sarah to the rustic sensibility of tench fishing was squashed.
My list of bands off Island samplers meant nothing to her either. She

didn't care for Traffic or Spooky Tooth. For her, nature was the muse and music was played by classical guitars and cellos in the arms of Segovia and Jacqueline du Pré. She fetched her guitar and sang to me then, plucking it like a cat scratching on a rug, her voice folky-throat, skimming in high, thin clouds, songs she wrote herself with lines like *bone comb for a lover*. She read me one of her poems before I knew what was happening. It was like she'd kissed me or like being sung to sleep when you're ill, perfect peace within a fever: *My life walks endless circles in the pouring rain.* . . Inside the house, Mr Jeffery was playing a Bach Brandenburg on a Baroque recorder. It was drifting through the open windows as I left *Almeida*, despising my previous sixteen blind, deaf years, half of them spent with a fishing rod. We all give up fishing. The first time is the best, usually for a girl and her poetry.

That same evening at home, I searched through my school exercise books. We'd done poetry with Mr Woolley in the fifth. This had consisted of copying out poems from books in the school library and altering the last half of each line. I chose one and phoned Sarah, eager as a dog who'd found something putrid in a dustbin. I read it down the phone. Of all the poems in the world I could have picked, I'd bowdlerised T. S. Eliot's 'Rhapsody on a Windy Night', lines from which Sarah had read me an hour before. She was generous, after blurting *You didn't write that.* My bluffing was artful, though. On my second trip to Ockley Pool, I'd had to rig up the rod myself for the first time. A fresh red quill I'd stolen from Woolworth's in Rye. I'd put it on upside down and the others split their sides. No, I'd said, it's a new kind of float. It doesn't go *under* when you've got a bite, it comes up.

Nineteen seventy-one became the summer of puppy love. The curtains fell from my eyes and I was blinded by sight. Under Sarah's guidance, and the Ordnance Survey map she always carried, Hawkhurst became transfigured, from a kind of open borstal of the over-familiar, into a new world of rustic vocabulary and pastoral verse. Places once designated for a laugh were now traversed by bridal paths, drovers' ways, jossing-blocks, cuckoo gates, spiles, wents and throws. Our romantic tramping filled by undertones from history and pagan tales. Streams and ponds, no longer targets for floats and worms, became the tapestries in Sarah's medieval landscapes, aesthetic bowers where she taught me nature's raw poetics. I became a cultural novice whilst Hawkhurst rebuilt itself under my feet. Instead of time melting in the sun, the past came into view and memory was the playing field of choice. Sarah brought my own past to life, a past I hadn't known was there; dreams which needed her interpretation, done deeds reviewed through the teachings of Freud, Marx, Jung. We walked down Roman roads, past Saxon manors, the cottages of Flemish weavers, behind Victorian breweries, over smugglers' tunnels, where the astronomer lived who named Uranus, the businessman who invented the Oxo cube. My village was at once a layered dream of knowledge and a blank page. The Hawkhurst I'd believed in for sixteen years had been demolished by Sarah in a day. The boy who'd lived a parallel life there had been expunged from its lanes and fields. And when I stumbled on the meaning of this, Sarah was there to show me how, through the consciousness of language, to feel the rain, watch a tree, listen to the words of birds. The fishing rods, for by now I owned six, became interred in shame, in the outhouse cemetery, with the cannon-ball, Mac's tools and the dog's box.

A novice is always disturbed by immensity. The sombre notes, the undertones, were in Sarah's own poetry. It wasn't an ordinary sadness. My early sense of being locked out of her poetry intellectually eased, through reading the collections she lent me. Instead, into that disturbance, came a fear that I would lose her to the very thing driving these precocious and brilliant poems. We saw each other every day, learned to kiss and walk miles arm in arm without tripping over our gowns and tie-dyed fancy dress, but all the time our happiness didn't seem as strong as the sadness, or gloom, in her poems. Then one morning she took me off on a short walk over the Lawns behind Theobald's Pond, where, I now knew, the Hawkhurst Orchestral Society had given concerts in their Edwardian heyday. She had something to tell me, something, she said, which would make me despise her. I feared that maybe I wasn't the first to have put my hand up her smock, but no, it was an invisible hand which had been there first. *I had depression*, she said.

Perhaps depression wasn't a poetic enough word. Sarah over-estimated how far I'd got with poetry if she thought I'd despise her for it. It was cold fear went through me instead. Until then, my progress had depended upon emulation. My fear was losing her to someone else, not invisibility. Ignorance runs so much deeper than wisdom. Everything she said to me was still new, previously unknown, and now this, another truth to diagnose. I had never been depressed for a minute of my sixteen years. But Sarah, at the age of fourteen, had spent several months in Bethlem Royal, a notorious psychiatric hospital. The rumours had been true. *They had to send her away.* She made it sound like a great public school for sensitive genius, where great poets and artists had suffered for their art. There, she'd read Sylvia Plath and forged her solidarity with fellow 'lunatics' Louis Wain, John Clare, Christopher Smart, Richard Dadd, Ezra Pound, Robert Lowell. She'd watched a girl set light to herself on the hospital steps. She took walks with a printmaker who starved herself to death. Sarah made the knowledge of such things seem as essential to a poet as the first trout is to a fisherman.

The correct response eluded me. I attempted something like: that's all right, I've been depressed too. She walked off shouting. *No, you don't understand. I mean real depression, suicidal depression.*

Even the intellectual is manual labour for a working-class youth. By September the worm had barely turned, a maggot hardly hatched. I was a poet, but I was Sarah's cultural slave, doggerel in the manger, still confused by this insistence on melancholy which love and poetry seemed to demand of us. Sarah began her last year at TWIGGS, in the fifth form. I enrolled at West Kent College of Further Education in Tonbridge. I'd left Swattenden with more roach over the pound mark than CSEs. O levels were for the elite, not the done thing at Swattenden, which had ceased educating anyway, flattened by the rise of the comprehensive. I'd been its last ever expulsee.

Sarah had procured the West Kent prospectus for me. She was enrolling herself the following year for her A levels, those two-pound roach of the mind. I had a year to get the entry requirement, two O levels. There was no question of her going to study poetry without me. My present course was flatteringly known as pre-diploma business studies. Five crammed O levels: economic history, accounts, the principles of English law, statistics and British Constitution. Lectures were in the Territorial Army drill hall. Access was through the garage bay where armoured vehicles were left unguarded. The rooms were cramped and dark. The lecturers were shabby, depressed men with bleak medical futures. Hernia men, goitres and stomach trusses already.

Fishing had been so thoroughly extinguished. Instead, I'd filled two exercise books with upside-down floats; concrete poems which sank to the bottom with the corpses of childhood, First World War poems where Tommy rides a ghost train in Flanders, derivative boggeral and polluted intention, the crude approximations of anything I read. The country was a part-time influence, the silent end of a day. Between 8.30 a.m. and 6 p.m., the towns were my pools and streams of knowledge. Such unfished territories, Tunbridge Wells and Tonbridge public libraries, teeming with books in unimaginable quantities. These I devoured in a poetry binge, the risked obesity of the autodidact. I read Ezra Pound's *Cantos* in accounts, while sweaty Simms in his pink nylon shirt explained the new giro cheque system; I read Sylvia Plath in statistics and Ted Hughes in Brit Con, under the desk or behind my green fishing haversack, now the repository of ring binders and mouldy text books. It's a feature of giving up fishing that you find yourself, in your neutral state, near better fishing waters than you have ever known. Tonbridge had the Medway. I saw it daily, wide, brown and alien. I felt sorry for the men who angled there. My glance was an unpleasant one. They hadn't read Pound or Eliot. They weren't going out with Sarah Jeffery. They might have said away with you then, you have to be worthy of the waters you fish.

On winter nights I passed through a hole in the hedge, the enchanted bypass, a secret passage between All Saints and Mercers. In three minutes I switched worlds, the class traveller. From Mac and Don's front-room mortuary, where the dog wheezed and dripped on a sheet of newspaper in front of the one-bar electric fire, to Connie and Arthur Jeffery's Bach- and book-filled chalet-bungalow, where the cat was called Calico and Sarah had a music stand and Modigliani postcards on the wall of her bedroom. A year of clumsy learning, blistering acne, atrocious poems, general ridicule at college for the hybrid freak virgin in the home-made flares. For Sarah it was a year of coming top in class and winning the school poetry prize for 'Aunt'. By now she was writing like Tony Connor and Ted Hughes and using words like 'façade' and 'pseudo', possibly with me in mind.

We learned enough to guess that it was true puppy love and couldn't last. That if I was lucky it would permutate, bed down, sink under circumstance and lay there preserved like an Elizabethan wreck or bog-man. Puppy love gets drowned in a rain barrel if you're extra lucky. Near the end, Sarah still needed what she'd learned from our time together. We wrote the *Brodie's Notes* on it, after all. Her lunchtime reading moved away from Eliot and on to Freud, her bedtime reading ditched Dylan Thomas for D. H. Lawrence. I'd become her literature practical, her *prol,* while she was my *bourgie.* To be fair, she was an Earl Grey Marxist, a Scholl and Shloer socialist who spurned her own kind of *bourgies.* She took me like a little lamb to school, but when I'd learned enough to start A levels neck and neck with her, she took me to the abattoir. Virginity of the brain. It had been fun, our private language, till that old cross-cultural crisis, birthright versus the struggle in Tunbridge Wells. The relationship just wasn't going to survive that kind of dialectic. Sarah was one huge pregnancy. I was a walking vasectomy. She was the projected slide, I was the undeveloped negative. Welterweight petting had been our limit.

In the first term of A levels we split asunder. Sarah prepared her retreat, switched classes, resigned from the Poetry Society, then relationshipwrecked us. She needed space, she was suffocating. In fact she torpedoed us in a storm. From inseparability to estrangement. She was offered a daily lift to Tunbridge Wells in a yellow mini with the postman's wife, a mature secretarial student who lived down All Saints Road. It left me an hour on the double-decker alone, jeered at from the back seats by City and Guilds mechanics or old phlobbers from Swattenden on a sandwich course for the GPO. She wouldn't see me in the evenings, despite my entreaties from the trunk call kiosk outside the bus station. At dinnertimes she ate her cottage cheese in the music room with the Virginias and Lucindas. The Jolyons and Piers drove their Mini Coopers to the Sussex where they quaffed pints of Newcastle Brown over a ploughman's. I slogged down to the penny book box outside Hall's, then sat on a bench in the Pantiles with a cheese roll, a bag of Golden Wonder and a Kit-Kat. I epitomised the class difference now, not the class struggle.

I had my first poems published around then, like putting on make-up after having acid thrown on your face. There had been an advertisement, in the *Sunday Express* probably, *Poems wanted for new anthology. No money to pay. Janay Publishing Company.* A vanity press, you bought a minimum of five copies of other books by the vainglorious in the pyramid. The result was three poems in *Gems of Modern British Poetry Volume 2.* Sarah was not impressed, quite rightly too, and the gesture failed. I had brought poetry into disrepute.

Sarah had already written a hundred pages of a novel. Whatever happened to her, she would always be the guitar-playing, cat-loving, cottage industry; mothering novels and poems and pies and pottery, singing to herself as she went. She'd said to me: *Well, what are* you *going to be?* I had no idea there was a choice yet. Family heritage in the working class was something Sarah couldn't grasp. The pointlessness of trying, the failure on the doorstep, the cruel magnitude of example. The way you have to lie your way out of a mess if you're born looking at the ground.

One winter evening, I dialled her number from the bus station telephone kiosk. Mrs Jeffery was always kind and polite, the jaunty hello, the *yes I'll just fetch her for you* voice as if nothing had happened. Not even when she'd been commissioned to make excuses. *Sarah's washing her hair. She's baby-sitting for the Jenners. She's doing her essay.* This time Sarah came to the phone, in a rage.

'What do you want?' she said.

'I must see you, please.'

'Why? Why should I see you? You'll see me tomorrow in sociology. Can't you talk to me then?'

'But it's not the same. We're never alone any more. I'm so unhappy, I just want to see you, that's all. We can go for a walk, I promise I won't annoy you. We can discuss our Lawrence essays. . .'

'Oh, all right. I feel like a walk, so.'

The magic word was *Lawrence. The Selected Poems of D. H. Lawrence* was on the syllabus. The first essay was due.

It was a crisp night, cold and starlit. We met at the crossroads. I was in my poet's kit, black loons, horsehair hacking jacket, Dr Who scarf, desert boots and silver-topped cane. Sarah had a Victorian fur coat, a long, grey skirt over knee-length platform boots and a grey, knitted woollen hat.

'You look beautiful,' I said.

She ignored the remark, then warned me that one snip of self-pity and she'd turn round and go home. We set off down Cranbrook Road and turned in past Pullen's. Conversation on her side was neutral, bookish, Freud, Desmond Morris. Mine was the sly poet, angling for that chink of hope. She anticipated this and shut me down each time I wandered off the subjects she set herself. At Gills Green we shunted right, past Dr Barnardo's Babies Castle into the lane towards the Dump where Hawkhurst's rubbish went in a landfill and Mick the Pig had his scrapyard.

'I've been working on my Lawrence essay,' she finally said. 'Have you done yours?'

It was the moment I'd been dreading, my first intellectual defiance of her poets. She devoured Lawrence, revered him above all writers. I loathed him with all my heart, half contempt at his clumsy writing and half jealous at the weight of his balls in his hand and their threat to Sarah's virginity. It was like he was a pop-up genie in each of his novels, a rough ghost pouncing on grammar-school girls, not the pigeon-chested, bearded dead dog responsible for Sarah's latest word *sensuality.*

'I didn't stick to the title,' I said, 'and I'll tell you why.'

'Go on then, tell me why.'

'It was idiotic.'

'Is that all you can say? That's not constructive criticism.'

'All right, we're supposed to discuss his poems. One of them's 'The Piano'. Well, it goes *taking me back down the vista of years, till I see a child sitting under the piano. . . In spite of myself* blah-blah about a song *betrays me back, till the heart of me weeps to belong to the old Sunday evenings at home, with winter outside and hymns in the cosy parlour. . . The glamour of childish days is upon me. . . I weep like a child for the past. . .'*

'So what's your point?'

'It's utter drivel!'

'Why? How can you say that? Just because you don't weep for your past.'

We'd walked under the last streetlamp some way back and were in darkness when Sarah turned abruptly on to an unpaved lane. She was already cutting the walk in half, taking a short cut in anticipation.

'Is that all you've written? That it's drivel? I thought you were all for objective criticism. You should question the images not dismiss them.'

'I bloody did. I gave it another title: *The Divergent Self*, and argued you can't be objective about Lawrence because he's subjective and contemptuous of women. He's just using you. You know what he said? *Any woman who says to me do you really love me deserves my undying detestation.* He's self-pitying, inconsistent and undisciplined. He's corrupting you.'

'Oh shut up!' Sarah said. 'You should have stuck with the essay title we were given.'

In the distance, I heard a familiar murmur. For the moment debased, diminutive. A dog barked as we clattered through puddles, briefly lit up from lamps inside an open barn.

'The whole course is useless,' I said.

The murmur became a stifled roar. We entered a band of mist, rolled out along the miniature valley. It was Ockley Pool, foaming in the moonlight like a rabid dog. Sarah leaned on the bridge, staring into the years from whence I'd come. She had played the ultimate Lawrencian punch line on me, *taking me back down the vista of years,* till I wept like a child for the past. Longing for lost simplicity is like an asthmatic fighting for air. I remembered my first trout, slipping it back, the swelling in the throat.

'I want to fall at your feet,' I said.

'Please, don't start.'

'It's all right, I won't. I just wanted you to know.'

She knew it word for word, listening to me with clenched fists at her side.

'Look,' she said, 'I don't want to talk to you any more. I'm serious.

Please leave me alone at college. I'm going home now and don't try to follow me.'

I stood staring down the chute, watching the darkness whirl inside the mist. Sarah was gone. Something had held me back from saying *Look, this is where I caught my first ever fish*. Was it because to her a trout was only a quartet by Schubert? The stars were like the thousand spots on a trout; the trout were like falling stars arcing with the flow. Why had I ever fished? It had seemed such a good and comforting thing, now so fragile, unspoken and yes, corrupted.

Dr Lewis was the family bones. His surgery at Northgate was a weatherboard cottage with leaded windows opposite the colonnade, its flagstone path beside cherry trees and copper beeches. He wore a sports jacket with leather elbow patches and drove a blood-sample coloured MG open-top on house calls. He was an all-day smoker, always had a Guards pluming in the Roche ashtray during appointments. A pocketful of fountain pens leaked ink blains on the tweed jacket hanging on the back of his chair. In the post-war modern sense, he was that old-fashioned believer in a sympathetic ear curing nine-tenths of your ills because he knew the rest was merely keeping it steady. If you had a cold he wrote a prescription to the off-licence for a quart of whisky. And being friendly cost nothing back then. He always asked how your mother was, if your sister still worked for Colgate, if Mac still drove the Sunbeam. As a boy I'd watched our doctor play cricket with the shopkeepers for the Wednesday XI. He was a nippy bat. He played the game.

With me he batted defensively when I said I couldn't sleep. So shyly, like ordering your first half pint, I used Sarah's word: *depressed*. He then, and only then, prescribed. He'd already treated my acne, and this felt like a follow up, though I think we were both embarrassed. I came to believe in this melancholy, the auto-propaganda of the poems. After a fortnight on the pink anti-poems, I couldn't tell Lawrence from a trout. I slept through classes, dribbled on the bus home, then paced the night away circling an easel in my bedroom or thumping on the great iron Imperial typewriter Mac had let me use. He jawed wearily across the landing in the deads before dawn.

'Will you pack it in and get to bed! I'm having that typewriter back. It's nothin' but a nuisance.'

'I'm paintin'.'

'Paintin' my foot! Yer ma'n me can't sleep with you banging about. Now do as yer told or do I aff' ter come in there?'

You couldn't blame him. He had to rise at 6.30 for his shift up the Esso garage in a grey storeman's coat. His gaffer was yet another big-headed fool who made his life a misery. We heard about it every teatime. Our car was back to a face-grey Austin Square 1 with gearbox disease. Things couldn't get worse. The paint had now peeled off the kitchen wall and the bills were stacked against us. There was nothing left to sell except our souls. At night I began to sneak out the back door when they were asleep. I'd walk through the village, doing my *Under Milk Wood* practical, passing every house where girls lived. Alas, there were no lights on, no suffragettes circling their easels or Plathing on their own Imperials. No one to beckon out into my night. I'd come to love the nights, free to wander through all of imagination. In the Moor churchyard, I sat upon frosted Victorian tombstones, inventing the ghost of a soul mate and leaving poems for her, dated 1872.

When the cricket season was underway, Dr Lewis referred me to an expert on haunted poets. There was no need to tell my parents just yet, he said. It being June, my general malaise became specific, even if I couldn't name it scientifically. My low ebb had the whole summer to recede along the deserted shores of Hawkhurst. Three months solitary, Sarah just the other side of the hedge. Late one afternoon, I walked from college down to the outpatients' clinic at the Homeopathic Hospital in Tunbridge Wells. The expert on poetical youth came straight out with it first question.

'Do you masturbate?'

'No.'

'Oh come on, we all do!'

'Yes.'

'To what fantasy? Male or female.'

'Ockley Pool.'

The next question was trickier.

'Do you hear voices?'

'Yes.'

Of course I did, but these were just the poems whispering through the walls of their bell jar, or jabbering in troubled water as it flowed under the bridge, not Dr Goorney's paranoid inveiglers. As a precaution, he suggested I come stay *in a little place I run in the country.* He called it Farm Villa. He said I'd be able to paint in the sun lounge and *interact* with worried souls like myself. I imagined some convalescent residency for wounded artists, a great orangery of poets, all the Sarahs of this world singing and setting light to themselves. All ideas of university were scrapped; Farm Villa was where I needed to be.

Unprepared for the destination of his next Sunday drive, Mac said: 'This is a blow, son.'

On the map it was still Barming County Asylum.

Don bit her knuckles through a handkerchief.

'Why can't yer stay at 'ome where yer belong?'

Sarah said: *Don't be so stupid, you've not got depression,* and walked off.

Till the morning of my departure, it was never mentioned. Then my entire belongings went into that bubble of an Austin A30. Boxes of books, easels, my bottle and bones collection, all my paintings, some which had old fishing sandwiches and anti-depressant tablets glued to them. Two goldfish in a bowl, one dead on arrival. And for some reason, the same reason, enough fishing tackle to see me through the night.

Part Two

ELEVEN

WHEN LIAM WALKED in the foyer door asking to see me, I smelled the trouble I wanted. Liam was Marie Dillon's eldest, deeply Irish, all my height but dark skint-eyed and black haired, pinched white skin, wisps of teenage below his ear line. He wore grey and sniffed all the time, flobbed a lot, his mouth pursed with the weighing up of getting away with anything he cared to. On the swivel that day, Liam was. He said he liked everything on the run, said he lived where everyone lived, down on the grey council estate that went on forever along the River Medway there.

Liam had come up to Farm Villa, where his mam was a night nurse. Come for a laugh at my expense, I knew that, expected it, just from the look of him. He said straight off:

'Shaw's yer fishin' stoff, then.'

We moved over the buffed lino like a leak from humanity's tap. Through the indelible smell of mental wards, sour-side up. The three-in-one of cold piss, instant coffee and nicotine ghosts. My fishing stuff was beside my bed in the dormitory. I thought I could sell it for fag and tea money, to supplement the two quid a week pocket money we collected every Wednesday from the stats office. But there weren't many anglers in that place, the Barming County Asylum. The gear wasn't much either, but it was more than Liam owned. The best of that tackle of childhood, the bulk of treasured memories he could have for an extra quid.

Liam was impressed, whistling a sly jealousy which meant he was getting his hands on it. I was just one of his mam's nutters. He even said he wanted to buy it, only he was short of cash till payday. He was shrewd and jobless. He meant this as stage one in a con he'd done before, his mam the inside job. They were just rip-off queens, the nurses. Charge nurse Murphy told me to shut my face when I complained about the filching of my record player and two paintings. Irish, the lot of them, thinking it was a convent, not an acute admissions ward.

Liam fingered my spinners, swooshed my rods, then said my accent worried him. My fake accent that is, so faked it still wouldn't come off unless I scrubbed it with Low-Life soap. He was polishing me up for that fishing tackle by mentioning his mates, hinting I might join them in something going on. Talking faux-posh would get the piss took and maybe a kicking. So I dropped it back to Boy of Kent and poured three years of two-timing dignity down the bog with relief. Just stuck my fingers down the voice box and up it came like diced poetry. The place was doing me good.

'A' you allowed out this fockin plairce? Now, loike?' he said.

'Oh yeah, fuck 'em,' I said. 'Anyway, there's two hours before the noight shift.'

'Me mam's on tonight, any road. She's at 'ome nor. She juss got 'erself up. OK then, let's go, but can ya bring along that poike plug wi' them treble 'ooks on it? Show me mates an' stuff. Tanks.'

'Stuff' was one of Liam's all-purpose words. The other thing Liam wanted, after my pike plug, was stuff about girls, women, bits of stuff. Any easy shags, *you knaw, nymphos an' stuff.* His mam had said the hospital was packed with it, even the nurses, packed into cupboards during night break, running away with patients at weekends. I said I could introduce him to a girl I knew. Liam slammed me on the back and said:

'You're a pal, but dorn say nott'n to n'orn.'

Liam's house was in a grey pebble-dashed terrace among the gloomy rows where one estate joined another, like layers of dirt accumulated over the years. There were six Dillons in two bedrooms. Sam Dillon worked nights too, at the paper mills, eyes red and heavy. Nurse Dillon was just up, like Liam said, but she was fresh as a daisy, dyed blonde, pointed tits, talking dirty from shit to shift. She was glad to see me, but said don't be too late. Old Marsden was charge nurse that night.

It was a grey spring evening, drizzling but warm. Outside, we kicked a punctured football in the cinders back of the garages, then Liam showed off my pike plug to his brother Fin and his mate Scab. He made me feel so proud to own it, I let him keep it, after all. They showed me the ten acres of allotments between their estate and the River Medway. It was where they went fishing, at the back of these allotments at night, for eels. They sold the fookers for ten pence a pound.

We threw stones at each other for a while, then Liam said they were going off, stuff to do. I had to ask his dad for a lift back. On the way, Nurse Dillon said:

'Liam likes you.'

I fixed him up with Angie two days later. He promised to take me night fishing if I did.

'Snot the fishin' season,' I'd said.

'Fock the season. Eels don't count. It's a good laugh, oi tell ya. There's cash in it.'

Angie was from another ward, way across the grounds where they housed the sprawling mad, patients from suburban catchments, Croydon, Sidcup, Slade Green. We were the country disturbed, the Maidstone & District bus-route nutters. Angie was a red-bus hermaphrodite who looked and dressed like David Bowie. She was halfway through her second year in art school. Her drawings were troubled, album-cover gothic, fantasy, creatures, warriors, broken columns, sweeping skies, hounded chariots flashing like lightning. She drew herself in fine pencil, such perfect lines, perfect likeness, manacled to a tree shaped like a witch's hand. Coming from Lewisham, she sounded like all my cousins. She stood in the car park outside Farm Villa in the rain every day until I went out with her. Just gritting up our flares in the wet, slogging round the grounds, sitting in the patients' canteen or shoplifting down Maidstone.

One night there was a disco on Female Nines, a long-stay ward. Angie and me went over there, ate sausage rolls and took the piss a bit. The nurses danced with old hags, making their arms go up and down to

Paul McCartney crap on an old Philips record player on the floor. Angie was weird, not me-type weird in Liam's eyes, but scary, jagged weird. I wanted to dump her before she cut my throat. After the disco we stood under the iron fire escape in the rain and lit up No. 10s. An hour to go before night medication. She wouldn't stop talking, a thousand words a minute. I was fungling her and smoking at the same time. I chucked the nub down and levered both her tits out. She was staring into the lamps and the rain, like I wasn't there, yattin' and yattin'. Then she was singing some new song she'd just heard by 10 cc:

Ah'm nod in la-arve, s'doan forgeddit, 's juss a silly phase ah'm goin 'frew. . .

As she sang the last verse I cried and scubbed myself against her till I dampened the Wolseys.

'Less go back now,' I said.

She hadn't noticed anything. It was early May, windy drizzle, blowing hot and cold. A foot in two seasons, the kind of day I caught my first chub on a fly down Bodiam, on the cane rod, with the old fly line Mr Cavey had given me. I remembered it because I'd felt on the verge of something, a twelve-year-old achieving a thing incredibly sensible. This was the furthest off I could think of. The furthest off I wanted to be right then. A boy who knew who he was in a world where the horizon stopped where it was supposed to stop. I'd even tied the fly myself, and maybe if I'd hung on to the pride, I wouldn't have gone the wrong way down a No Through Road, heard the poetry voices or wasted these moments in a psychiatric hospital. Eighteen years old and going with Angie down the slope to an impurity where neither words nor water flowed. I knew that once you lost hold of the fishing, just being working class was like having epilepsy a hundred years ago. They bunged away the key so you had to keep filing at the bars. The screech it made drowned out the fading songs which Sarah had convinced me were there.

We walked over the grass and stopped just outside the ring of light from Farm Villa. Angie laid down on the wet grass and said:

'Yer c'n screw me up t' the eyeballs tomorrer. I'm flyin' the red flag today.'

I told Liam. He said:

'OK, oi wouldn' moind a bidda groin.'

He took me eel fishing in the middle of May as promised. Liam's mam was on duty. She fixed it so I could stay out all night, unnoticed by the charge nurse. There was me, Liam, his brother Fin and his mate Scab. On the way down to the river we raided the allotments and rooted up several old fence posts for firewood. Scab busted into a shed and wogged a can of paraffin to get the fire going. We had the billy kettle too and I'd grabbed handfuls of teabags and a fresh white Sunblest from Farm Villa kitchen. Scab said he only ate stuff his mam could nick from work.

Liam had advised me to bring a minimum of tackle, in case we had to leg it. All they had was a rod each, a bucket, and a carrier bag with their stuff in. I had two rods, a tackle box and a landing net. They were all over it before we even got there, borrowing tackle I would never get back.

They showed me what to do when it was dark and the fire was lit. We had weak torches. We kept having to bounce them off the ground to get them to come on again. What they did was kid's stuff. You threaded a big drilled bullet or coffin lead up the line, stopped it with a swan shot, tied on a big hook and baited it with a bunch of worms. Liam said you didn't want *focken bootlaces* to grab it and run off in ten directions with the one worm. You could get four lobworms on a big size 2 rusty sea hook. *Big bastards you're after*, he said. *Two bob eels. Packet o' fags every toime you get a boite.*

They snapped prods off bushes for rod rests and we all cast into deep-brown sluggish water. A great clonk of leads and a clish of knotty coiled lines compacted from years of misuse. Their rods were solid glass spinning rods with the top eyes missing or a good foot snapped off. Liam borrowed one of mine and both my rod rests.

The river was wide there, the paths worn flat, dog mess and litter, dead fires and Durex in all the swims. We sat in the fire glow, the rods all propped up high with sea-fishing bells clipped to the tips, little pet bells attached to clothes pegs by a spring. Then one of them dinged off, shaking like a baby with a rattle. We all ran to the rods shining our torches up in the air.

'A-hey, it's moine lads,' Liam said, waiting for the bell to rittle again before he struck. 'Yez, focken on. Jeez, big 'un, Scab.'

His reel handle fell off and he dragged the eel in by walking up the bank. It slapped the ground so Scab put a foot on it.

'Swallered the 'ook,' he said. 'Give it a rip.'

'Naw, where's the knoife?'

Liam cut the line and chucked the eel in the bucket. We all looked. It curled twice round the bottom.

'Twenny-foive pee that one.'

I caught eleven eels that night. Liam gave me fifty pence and kept the rod and all my weights. I took the money to Maidstone market and bought a pair of platform shoes. Behind the stall was the river where we'd fished. The shoes were the latest fad, moulded plastic, two-tone red. I put them right on and chucked the desert boots in a bin by the river. My drainpipes were jumble sale, lawyer's pinstripes. They didn't go with the platforms, but it was too late to get the boots back. Going modern had to hurt, and looking a prat was the price of avant-garde. I walked like a horse in stilettos up the main Tonbridge Road. Passing drivers shouted out their windows, calling me an oil rig, asking if I was on the stage or if my husband knew I was at work.

By the time I reached the hospital gates, my crippled feet bled. Liam was there waiting, moved to fury when he saw the shoes. He said I couldn't go fishing with his mates looking like a clockwork robot. I had better just lend him the rest of my gear.

'No way,' I said. 'I'ad to buy these shoes coz you only gave me fifty pee fer them eels.'

He said fair do's. I could earn some more, but I'd have to wear his football boots, he didn't have another pair of shoes.

It was a Friday night. Liam said we'd have to be ready to leg it this time. There was going to be a fight in town, it was all arranged, skinheads were coming up from Rochester. There were other eel fishers in the dark and word spread along the bank that twenty skins were working their way from the town end, kicking rods in. Liam said I'd be all right, I just had to kick 'em back with his football boots. We were only half a mile from the market stretch so when we heard the shouting we packed in and legged it to the allotments. Fin was dropping live eels on the way, trying to stop them snaking off into the grass. Some skins got hold of the kids just round the bend from us. They chucked them in the river and kicked shit through their gear. We lobbed our stuff over the allotments fence and lit it up Liam's house, giving it an hour till the police came along. We got the gear back when it was quiet and even caught five more eels, but Liam threw up after eating a whole Hostess Roll and a bottle of cherryade he'd nicked from his mam's cupboard. The police came along at dawn and took our names and addresses.

'Hell's bells,' the copper said. 'Three tinkers an' a nutcase.'

They were talking of chucking me out, the nurses. They were doing the assessments and said I showed no signs of any depression they'd ever heard of. Every day now, Pat Murphy, who was charge nurse on days, said he knew my game. He was a sharp Alec, said I was a con and you can't win at losing. I had to throw them off the scent because I was enjoying this eel fishing. The doctors had taken their eye off me. Psychiatrically, I was of no clinical interest. After group therapy stopped for morning coffee, I was free and unsupervised. The staff considered fishing occupational therapy, natural valium. I was going to the Medway independently of Liam now. The alternative was back home with Mac and Don, where I would have to get a job. I'd already been discharged twice, but after a month in All Saints Road I'd staged some amateur dramatics to obtain re-admission. Now, every time Pat Murphy saw me, he pointed to the door and cut his throat with an index finger.

The only way to obtain an extension was to fake a suicide attempt. Half the patients were at it and we knowingly called it para-suicide. You gained four weeks observation or the benefit of the doubt. One night I walked into town and tried to find some portion of the river where I could simply baptise myself without danger, being a non-swimmer. The river was hungry and the streetlamps made it look greasy and ready to suck me under. I found an ornamental rock garden instead, hidden behind some bushes, a little tumbling stream and a pool like a washbasin. I took my fags out to keep them dry, then drip by drip I wet myself, scooping the water timidly on to my head and clothes until I thought I looked authentically at peril.

The police station wasn't far off. I went up to the desk and said I'd tried to drown myself, but somebody pulled me out then ran off. I was put in a side-room and given a blanket. There was hardly any dripping on the floor. A detective came in and took one look.

'You're that bloody stupid eel-fisher. Show us them fags.'

Five Sovereigns, all dry as tinder.

With a new set of weekly motivation targets, I was sent to the Industrial Huts and put to work packing Plasticine strips and tying Remploy labels on to three-pinned plugs. The irony did not escape me. They smartened me up too: a haircut, fresh clothes, and insisted I take my first ever shave. For this I was issued with the Farm Villa electric shaver and expected to accomplish it alone. It ploughed instead of harvested. A young post-graduate was on his bed outside the bogs, where he spent most of his days. All the while he kept up a monologue about how he couldn't wank any more because of the medication. When I stepped back into the dormitory he laughed himself sillier than he was. My hideous new face. Gone was the bumfluff beard of the Pre-Raphaelite pretender. In its place a slash-up. I'd cut myself all over with an electric razor. He said I'd joined the ranks of the female patients who got their tampons stuck and had to call a nurse with a rubber glove.

The shave was not entirely cosmetic. It had a deeper reason. The date was June 15th and the fishing season began at midnight. The Remploy labels had set off thoughts of Mr Cavey, of Risden and its tench. My mind was helplessly adrift. I recalled each time I'd fished the opening day of the season, the all-consuming joy of it. Those carefree dawns as the sun rose on an empty page. Twice, I'd been waterside at midnight on the 15th, like a secret gathering handed down. You assemble on the eve and count the minutes till the first cast at zero hour. Sarah would have called it a pagan act of celebration, a sacrifice of bread flake in the light of a rusty torch. It was more than a yearning now. I wanted, needed, to be at Risden; hypnotically drawn to go there and cast into its waters at midnight.

Yes, I suspected it was the inner voice of a drowning man wishing he'd learned to swim. Perhaps it was time pulling me back to a land without the complications of poetry. Nothing in Farm Villa, the abattoir of thought, was making much sense. Inmates spoke of 'the outside world' when remembering their past. I supposed I'd become institutionalised, but I wasn't convinced this was a lucid moment either, or that any pilgrimage to Risden was even a good idea. It was too like begging fishing for another chance. And it was going back, something all the Pakistani psychiatrists I'd been seeing of late had pet words for.

The bus, a number 5 double-decker, arrived in Hawkhurst at teatime. Don and Mac were more worried by my arrival home than my latest re-admission. Mac even phoned the hospital to check I had overnight leave. He kept saying:

'You all right, boy? You sure, in yerself, like?'

I was regretting it by then. The spare tackle I'd left in the shed was manky. The line on my reels was rotten. The tackle-box hinges had rusted away. I'd brought my hospital rod and reel, but Liam had pocketed most of my decent sundries. There was no time to sort it out. I bolted my tea and took what there was. Back in commission, the fishing haversack bulged from the additional flask of Typhoo, three cream crackers and a lump of cheese. I ran for the bus, sweating in a pair of light baggy flares, old football socks, nylon shirt, tank top and spare v-neck. The outdoor gear made all the difference: desert boots and Mac's old anorak. Two irritated parents washed up the silence I'd left behind.

'Bit queer this sudden fishin',' Mac had said. 'There's no need to go fishin' of a sudden an addin' to needless worry.'

The last number 84 dropped me at Field Green. I waded in twilight across the field, plunging into thick darkness under the trees. This was not the picture I'd had of it in Farm Villa. I rooted the cycle lamp out from the bottom of my haversack. The lamp squeaked on and went bright when I smacked it twice. Half the cracked glass fell out. I could smell myself, the sweat and effort of tackling-up on my knees with cramp and twitching eyes from the anti-depressants. Withdrawal symptoms already. I should have taken my night medication an hour ago.

I cast the legered worm out about midnight. Don only had a farmhouse crust to spare, but I did manage to cast a float without the paste flying off. Then, for half a minute, the old excitement gripped me. The float danced in the lamplight. I even kidded myself I might land a great tench, settle old scores, get back to that point before things went wrong with Sarah.

She'd reappeared in Hawkhurst after a year of psychology at Warwick had disappointed her. We took walks to Bodiam, picked blackberries and picnicked in the rain. It was October. One evening there was mist over the barley stubble and we'd filled our pockets with chestnuts, lit a fire and roasted them in an old rusty tin. She'd said she was leaving Hawkhurst for good and wanted me to go with her. She was confident, impatient for more life. I was still circling the old one, and the poems had fallen silent. *Go where?* I'd asked. *Anywhere,* she said. Hastings, Wales, Kettering, Hampshire, Devon, she didn't care. She'd waited two weeks for me to think it over, mounting her argument daily, describing my bleak future alone like a clairvoyant. Over and over, I asked her what we'd do. She said we'd find a flat, get jobs, write in the evenings. *Damn it,* she eventually said, *make your mind up, I'm not waiting any longer.* Someone else had asked her to live with him in Ilford, so would I just pull myself together and do it. She'd left it up to me; I'd been, at that moment, her first choice, not her second. He was a safety net, a dull fellow who would provide for her. He programmed punch-card computers and she'd met him on a geography field trip back at college. His presence had narrowed my vision of the outside world. All I could imagine was living in some noisy bedsit above an off-licence, the streetlamp streaking through the thin curtains and the lorries waking me up. So when she'd come for my final answer I said no. I knew it was the wrong answer, after all that bloody effort. Cultivating a mind then smashing the greenhouse, the failed A levels, and now the poxy nutter scum I was hanging out with, *Diamond Dogs* day and night on the Farm Villa hi-fi, tea in the patients' canteen with female axe murderers. Sarah hadn't waited any longer. When the two weeks expired, she'd left and married Mr Second Best.

At one minute past midnight I took in my surroundings and thought of the long night to come. I felt the cold now, the cold of being so uselessly alone. A quick cup of stomach-churning grey tea from the stale thermos failed to mend the broken moment. I was wobbling on a fold-up garden chair, bright orange flowers on rent nylon. The cycle lamp scared off the fish, making us both blind. I could be surrounded by pikeys or farmers and not know it. And supposing I hooked a big tench? Lost, the way I'd lost Sarah, in the dark. The snapping line like a pistol shot, the last line in a Russian play, *Constantine has shot himself.* The torch beam was a signal to my enemies. The pikeys would come now. Mac or Don would tell Mr Cavey. There would be shame both sides of the fence.

Three fags left. The hair stood up under my shirt when a badger screamed behind me. I bashed the lamp off. The bobbin knocked on the leger rod, something tugged at it like a poltergeist. A crashing in the rhododendrons had me whimpering at the tench to get lost. It was time to scarper. A swipe at the cycle lamp only sent it into the lake. The beam flickered back on a second to light its way down till the silt snuffed it out with an air bubble. I slung the leger in the grass and left the bail arm open. The tench could swim about all night if it had to. Sod the float rod. There were shapes all around me, shifting back and forth, bushmen and scarecrows come to life.

The all-consuming joy of opening night was escaping from it, speed-walking to the open field, into a cold sea of mist under half a moon, through ankle-snagging brambles, the face-high scratches like a back-hander across my newly tilled skin. Tired and cold, I curled up in the middle of the field and smoked two Sovereigns tip to tip. I had no courage left to go back and fetch the flask. It was 4 a.m. when I awoke, teeth chattering, tiny spiders up my nose, the damp like sweat from fever. I smoked the last fag and stamped up and down to rid the numbness and the cold.

Back at the lake, I had my answer. Whatever angling spirits exist to be offended, I had deserved their offence. My tackle box was emptied over the ground just to show contempt. They hadn't wanted any of it. The reel was missing off the leger rod. The bottom was missing from my life. Well you could stuff fishing. I was back in Farm Villa by dinnertime. The cleaner saw me come in and said: *Didn' know you was a fisherman.*

TWELVE

AT NINETEEN YOU TAKE THE EASY ROAD to self-deception, a smooth slipway with no speed limit. Fishing was the only ticket out of Hawkhurst on a Wednesday afternoon. Away from parents still worried sick, the blinds drawn on closed shops, the British Legionnaires with dewdrops taking flowers up to the cemetery. Adolescence had come home to roost with Mac and Don, then abruptly tumbled into a heap of brown Terylene flares with no other reason to get off the bed. The River Rother still flowed through Bodiam, even if ambition did not. The number 84 bus might have changed its number to the 254, but it still ran with open arms in 1975.

One afternoon, I took the wicker basket and an ugly blue Olympic roach rod, its handle wrapped in ceiling-tile cork, purchased in Woolworths with my eel money. It was a platform shoe of a rod, thick as a pole-vault, a swing-tip screwed into the top eye like a broken chicken leg, thirteen floppy feet away.

I decided to leger without conviction, too anxious of Mac's next move to make me get a job in that work-a-day world of his. My spots had cleared up, I was turning into a man, a layabout man treating the house like a hotel. Jobs meant the petrol pumps, the lawn-mower showroom, the wood yard.

It was February, and by sheer fluke I pounded the bread flake on a shoal of hungry, unscrupulous, unemployed chub laying about under the bank downstream. I took fourteen over two pounds, the junior keep net bulging like a Christmas stocking. The biggest chub weighed 2lbs 12ozs. For once I was a specimen hunter celebrating success. For once there was truth and substance behind my angling declarations. Like always, inside the teenage prism, this one achievement was not satisfactory. By implication, it made all fiction dreamed up on the bed attainable. If I could actually catch chub like this, then I could have caught those other dreamed-up fish: the 11lb 4oz carp from Delmonden, the 4lb 10z tench from All Saints Pond. I filled in the Bodiam Angling Club catch forms and that year took the prize for second-biggest specimen chub and second prize for most specimens.

One chub makes a summer for a soul in winter. Other anglers were necessary to share this burgeoning ego. But where were they now? All those boys you used to fish with were also men. Only they were at work, or drinking in the public bar where it might be best you didn't go. You pull your own short straw. Art is over, the writing has spiralled into self-parody. You're living in a village with no friends; it's what happens when you jump the queue. The £9.64 a week benefit goes on twenty King Slims and more bus fares to oblivion. It won't stretch to a field of operation and you can't afford a barometer of personality yet.

Ignoring the voice of reason, I posted a letter to the *Angling Times*. *Specimen Hunter wishes to start Specimen Group*. The phone rang on the Wednesday night. The caller was suspicious as soon as I opened my mouth. My alter ego had shot out like a trapped moth from a hatbox, leaving gift of the gab to save a bad angler from a bird's nest. At last I summoned enough sense to listen. My caller was from Hastings, his mate was standing beside him. With remarkable assurance, he outlined both their pedigrees, their proven skills, a bulging repertoire of fish I had never dreamed of, a surfeit of gear I had never heard of. For the moment, they assumed I was on similar rations. I should have hung up or said wrong number, but I hung on, like a dumb roper on an airship, till I was too chicken to jump off without breaking my neck. My caller said there were actually three of them who had already considered starting a specimen group. We might combine. How many did I have? We were picking sides, tossing for captains already. I said three without hesitation, slapping the hibernating social skills like a rescued pit pony. GET UP TRUTH! MOVE! Who was there, even remotely serious about fishing in Hawkhurst? The shoal had moved on. Instead of fishing, they were tinkering with the Anglia all Sunday, taking their birds stock-car racing Saturday afternoons. All I could think of was Roger Daltry's milkman who fished in a Soviet army greatcoat, and his mate with the nice sister, a silent bloke who fished in a fawn duffle coat. I'd been at school with both of them, but we'd never been friends. We might have said *what cheer* if we passed on the street, not much else. They went fishing in a car, which to me meant serious venues, real waters where you couldn't not be specimen hunters, surely. Specimen hunting took place *outside* the Hawkhurst boundary. There were four-pound bream and tench in the Royal Military Canal, ten-pound pike in the River Beult. It must mean that.

Mark and Alan drove out to see me in a brown L reg Ford Escort, coast-town men apiece. Mark wore Levi's and a white roll neck, moccasins and spectacles. Alan was older, more of the sensible brown chords and anorak with his roll neck, flat hair and thick-rimmed glasses. Anticipating something of the sort, I kept my purple corduroys in the drawer and hid the silk scarf. I greeted them in a Simon & Garfunkel shirt and herringbone flares. But it made no difference. They'd come to put the mockers on me and it was *ooh, ducky* from the off, like Morecombe and Wise interviewing me for a job in a flower shop. Once they'd hit the weak spot, they were sharks basking in their own wit and pinning me in the corner of my own stupidity: *'Ow many doubles you say you'ad? What's yer best chub over four pounds? You eel fish with what? An orange cork on your line? Not still in the bottle, is it?*

The way they described it, theirs was evangelical fishing. Five-pound tench out of Carter's gravel pit in Rye, eleven double-figure carp from a reservoir called the Spoon in Hastings, two-pound snakes from ditches on the Romney Marsh, nine-pound wildies from on top of the cliffs at Fairlight, four-pound chub from Newenden. This was talk which left me feeling queer.

I palmed them my own legend. It was too late to pull out now. 11lb 4oz carp, Delmonden, floating crust. The exact same story Mr Cavey had given me, ill-gotten and laundered. The old rod a-bending, the old reel a-smoking. Suspecting a counterfeit, they wanted photographs and asked to see the rod. We were standing in my bedroom. The boy's tackle leaned against the wardrobe behind my back, scorned by gypsies, pillaged by Liam, looking like a job lot of relics in a jumble sale. I'd concealed the worst of it under the bed, along with all inconvenient signifiers of other lives: the straw dog, my Faber poetry collections, a few pen and inks, Airfix kits, ship in a bottle. But Mark saw through me:

'This your carp rod?'

He reached for the roach-conquering Milbro Caledonian, the original replacement of the cane rod. The rings had rusted up after ten years and even then it had hailed from another era. Mark stole a glance at Alan. Four rolling eyes and smirks in convoy, one going all the way round Mark's face.

'What's it for, growin' runner beans?'

'Is that your rod holdall,' Alan said, 'or a wind sock? Ha ha, sorry Dex, only jokin'.'

He slapped his leg. The same rod holdall from school, the same joke I'd received from the back seats of the school coach. They had standards, Alan said, and, still the double act, Mark pulled out a set of photo-flips, archives of their captures to keep me squirming, not necessarily from envy but the moribund laid out between us, the vacancy, my life once again gone speechless in the face of more unknowns. After the Instamatic prints of big carp, tench, eels, bream and roach, Mark unfolded a cutting from the *Angling Times*, a centre-page feature, Alan and Mark winter chubbing in the sleet on the River Rother.

'Show us your photos now, Dex,' Mark said.

My only photos were of a campsite in Calais, my Airfix kits in the grass out front, some flying specks at air shows, one of Jim Clark winning the British Grand Prix from behind someone's head, and Garry Reeves with a twelve-ounce perch. Thinking of Garry raised some hope. He'd lived next door to Don Ham in a small close of private houses behind All Saints pond. The only feature distinguishing them from ours was that their gardens weren't fenced in. Garry's mum used to cut my hair in her kitchen. Once his dad showed us an old sepia photo he kept in a hook wallet. Thirty brown wartime tench squirming in the grass, caught from a private lake in Eridge, the other side of Tunbridge Wells, a lake he wouldn't take us to. Fishing with Garry was always about hankering for his dad's 3lb tench while we pulled quarter-pounders from anywhere we could. Forlorn hope, the way we dreamed of playing at Old Trafford. Garry had worn nice cotton country shirts, but his football was knock-kneed and wayward at thirteen. Then they moved away. Six years on I played for the village team in the broken-laced mud, balls you avoided heading unless you'd already lost your brains all over the pitch. China Rhoades, the chimney sweep and coach, painted the match ball with white emulsion before every game. It never stopped the leather soaking up two pounds of floodwater. It was while I sank with the Hawks to the bottom of the East Sussex league that Garry signed up with Gillingham as a semi-pro, playing in the Fourth Division. One Sunday afternoon he was on the telly, twenty minutes of *Southern Soccer* highlights. Reeves, the eighteen-year-old winger who flew past half-backs to seven hundred rattles and blue rosettes. Where did all that grace suddenly come from? Who'd managed to coax all that latent talent from his pipe-cleaner body? My revelation clutched at straws; if he could become a footballer, then I could become a specimen angler.

I pulled Mark and Alan like a barge along the towpath of lies. And I parried, and promised. We could rent our own carp ponds off local farmers. A full set of specimen gear was arriving for the start of the season. My photos were at my gran's and soon I'd be getting a job. I said this, I said that, said nothing to set their minds, or my own, at ease.

We were six at the inaugural meeting in Hastings. I had great trouble persuading my two Hawkhurst pikers to turn up. They fell through the ice first cast, quite rightly upset by similar interrogations over the pedigree of their tackle and the standard of their catches. The piss taking, on home soil, was from the pike's mouth. It made Liam small fry. You should not tell blokes like Alan that your rods snap in half every time you hook a pike. Personally, I was relieved they walked out of the meeting or they would have dragged me under with them. We were now back to important matters of ego. I was voted secretary, Alan chairman, Mark treasurer, Royston some species of bailiff or bouncer.

Membership cards and headed stationery were printed. And this was the year all fishing tackle shops started calling themselves Angling Centres, so there was something in the air, changes taking place.

The wild card was Royston, Alan's cousin. He was also on the waiting list for the local Hell's Angels. Being a matter of some priority, it meant Royston might not have any time to fish in the coming season. He was one of those half-pikeys who would kill you if you looked at his sister. Long black hair, earring, slack chinned, coming on hard all the time. He hung out with the greasers on the seafront, and always looked like he'd just got up from sleeping under a leaking chopper. He drove a big bonneted slab of Vauxhall rust, a six-seater from the '60s. The chrome wings jagged like rusty bread knives, or just a wounded grin coming apart. He drove it, in his commando cap, like a jet fighter and had us all do moonies out the side windows.

Being the closed season, there was idleness. Alan had family responsibilities and debts. As company, he dropped by the wayside, just chairing the fortnightly meetings. He was older than us, a married man with a toddler and a mortgage on a new townhouse where the trees were still sticks with dog collars. He was a worried man, picking up short contracts as a water treatment engineer. He wasn't certain he'd be fishing that summer either.

One Sunday afternoon in April we drove to Essex in Royston's Vauxhall Tetanus to visit Del Romang. Electronic bite indicators were still largely unchanged from Dick Walker's wires and bulbs of the 1950s. The group all used Herons, screechy things with crude contact plates which often stuck in the night. Del Romang converted them, stuck a GPO speaker on the outside and improved the sensitivity. He lived in a bungalow where the front-room table was piled high with converted Herons awaiting collection or posting.

'Wow,' Mark said, 'this is the shape of things to come.'

Del Romang was twitchy we would see something we shouldn't. He hinted that there were things to come we had never dreamed of. Thirty-seven years later his name is on every carp angler's lips in the world, and half the bite alarms ever sold. And I was once a tadpole in his jam jar.

Mark, Royston and I were all signing on the dole. By the end of April we were playing the one-armed bandits on the pier and doing fifty-pence matinées in a pokey flea-pit watching films like *Scum* and *Borstal.* When the pub opened, we slumped over bummed fags and everlasting halves of bitter. I couldn't afford this life. The bus to Hastings twice a week, living on fish and chips, flea-pits and slot machines, one pound fifty keep for Don, fag money and the group kitty. By the time we muddled into the pub after killing another day, I was broke. All those vital pennies that should have equipped me for the specimen-hunter world frittered away. Mark would lick an imaginary pencil and add another round to my IOU. In pub ignorance, I drank lager and lime. They pissed themselves about that, mocked and parodied everything I said, or did. I was there for mirth, too enthralled by angling visions to stay away. Even when we pooled our boredom, their pools were better stocked than mine.

Normal strategy for close season blues in Hawkhurst was to go worming for trout in the tiny streams, or conjuring out coarse fish from the Rother on a fly. But the specimen group operated on town rules. They didn't know about such joys, and thus forbade the little sissy brown trout from consideration. We had bigger fish to fry. Instead, like playing air guitars, Mark and Royston re-lived their handful of double-figure carp from the Spoon reservoir on their air rods. In such moments, I felt like the colossal infiltrator I actually was. I would be doing up the desert boot shoelaces under the table, both eyes like spy cameras. I knew so little that I learned all I knew about playing carp just from watching them on their air rods. And I knew what was coming. My own eleven-pounder, curved air in a public bar. Like a captured minstrel, I was forced to go through it for their entertainment. Pub theatre, Basil Brush goes fishing. It became a regular item and turned more absurd, and more obscene. In the end they would bang on the table and shout for it. Any reluctance was met by veiled threats and debt reminders. There was nothing for it, I would have to perform or there would be no fags, no sandwich, no half a pint. Other times, in the fair weather, I would play the wandering minstrel, or a dancing caddy, scuffing round the crazy golf on the cliff-side. Always left out from the carp all-stars trophy because I couldn't afford the green fee. There was no shortage of contestants. Hastings was awash with unemployed 'schoolboys' like us, killing out the closed season dodging the social security snoops. Mark, Royston, Paul Saddler, Graham Kent. Anything was entertainment, and I was on the bill, a seaside matinée idolatry. First performances were halting and basic: from tackling-up to putting the carp back in the water. Even as a lie it was nothing special. Delmonden, half-acre farm pond, uncatchable four-pound wildies. I crept behind the reeds one evening, lowered a floating crust and waited. But each recital met with more stage directions. They demanded every turn of the knot, what was in my head on the walk from the bus stop, what kind of loaf the crust came from, who lived on the farm nearby, who the milkmaids were, had I shagged 'em?

For me the sin, the shame, was two-fold. Pinched from Mr Cavey, I hadn't even made the story up. After listening to Mark and Royston's true stories on the power of a carp, it was plain that my Milbro Caledonian was not a carp rod. Theirs were ten-foot hollow fibreglass Bruce & Walker Mk IVs with Mitchell 300 reels. Graham Kent's were stepped-up Gerry Savages. So I began to change the story. I had, I decided, borrowed Mr Cavey's ten-foot salmon-spinning rod and Intrepid Elite reel. The desecration of a sacred moment deserved appropriate equipment. Did I stop to ask myself how much it had cost him, telling me that story over the fence in his Sussex burr, of a better time, when he'd heard *them ole carp shlooping their fart lips under them ole lily pads*? No. Once profanity takes hold, you clutch it like a straw. There is no sympathy left for a man who tells you that once he'd caught his carp, he lost the desire to ever go there again. If I'd have stopped to think, I might have wondered if he meant the pond, or the memory. Because one day, I would have to do the same. Was that the true power of the carp?

My parody of Mr Cavey's version began to produce bawdy howls of laughter. The pressure to make them accept me as an angler temporarily diminished. Instead, I enjoyed this brief respect as a comedian and story-teller. My audience would even call their mates over.

'Give 'em the carp story, moosh.'

The story took on the impediments of next door. Me old tin leg, the Intrepid Elite with its shoe brush round the spool which I'd buff me leg with to a shine. It corrupted, fragmented into slapstick, into *Carry On Carping*, till the whole story had become a filthy, shaggy dog joke about a tin-legged man carp fishing opposite a brothel. He casts his hundred-yard cock through the window. As it nears its goal, a steamroller comes round the bend. Winding the reel till it smokes, the punch line even had Royston's greasers rolling under their bikes:

'An' there oi warzzz. . .'

In the midst of this descent through barbarism, everything overheard about fishing was memorised, like a prisoner eavesdropping for mention of the key. I was Mac's boy, double or quits this time. All I needed were a couple of ten-foot compound tapers, two Mitchells and a new landing net. Then I would be out there with them. I was already kipping two nights a week on the floor in Mark's bedroom with its wall-to-wall *NME*s and metal albums like pillars stacked either side of the door. The fat plastic photo-flips were a pillar in progress, all the fish he'd ever caught, shown to me so many times I began to dream about them at night. Before I had even touched a carp rod, I absorbed Mark's aura of specimen angler, the knowledge of the set-up, the interpretation of water, which in those days meant the margins. If you were calm, soft of foot, silent and graceful, you could be a carp angler. At night the carp were under your feet. You didn't need to go looking for them; you baited, waited, and chain smoked until they arrived.

When alone with Mark, I was his disciple, though he didn't know this. Without a pecking order, he was reasonable and the mockery ceased. My questions were not targets for sarcasm, but opportunities for quiet debate. His reservations were only skin deep, and my carp was a call sign, not digested truth: *You did really catch it?* he would half ask, leaving me an escape lane. I had caught one carp in my life, a two-and-a-half-pounder. My biggest fish were the tench from school and the chub which won me the postal order. Nevertheless, come June 16th I would have to appear on the bank as secretary of a specimen group, and fish like one who knew.

Royston's car was written-off, but he wanted to go to the Carp Anglers' Society AGM at Billing Aquadrome, outside Northampton. We had no money, so we hitched up the M1 together on the Saturday.

It was early May, the day of the FA Cup final. Man United had lost to Southampton. Hooligans were smashing up the M1 services and throwing bottles out of coach windows. Two Asians gave us a lift, tried to drug us, then dumped us on the hard shoulder when they realised we had no cash. We slept in a bus shelter in a pool of oil just outside Northampton. Billing was a symbolic venue, a place of early carp legends. Unheard of then, a brace of thirty-pounders in the sixties. Photos of a bloke in a mod anorak and a home-made landing net, big sideburns, fatter lips than the carp. I don't think I even saw the lake that weekend. Caravans blocked it out, a big clubhouse, lots of rain.

Peter Mohan was chairman of the CAA. He declared the meeting open, but two sentences into his speech a fellow in the third row leaned back in his chair and puked his fish and chips into a ten-foot cascade. The front three rows were hit. Carp anglers scattered on all sides. The meeting was suspended while the victims took showers in the toilets and carpets of newspaper were laid down. I joined the squeamish outside for a smoke. That's all I remember of the meeting.

We bummed a lift back south in the rear of Stablers tackle shop van. We filled our pockets with hooks and swivels. There weren't any other carp sundries in those days. The tackle shop was in Earlsfield, London, where they dropped us off at midnight. Royston said it was a laugh, till we walked all the way to South Bromley before getting a lift in a lorry. Down the A21, the driver ran at least a dozen rabbits over. He said night driving was boring if he didn't kill something on the way home.

I still walked a lot at night in those days, in all weathers, right through winter. That night, those last seven miles alone from Flimwell to Hawkhurst were the worst, though it was a fine May night. Another pair of second-hand desert boots and nylon socks worn down. It wasn't just the dead feet. I was a long way out by then, drowning in the nights. Poetry and love were just the effluent and flotsam washing past, out of my life and gone. It was 4 a.m. I would be twenty years old next month. I had no clothes in which to go to the ball. Already, the others were loading up their 300s, waxing their Bruce & Walkers, airing out the NATO tank suits, and pre-baiting the Spoon with every penny of their dole cheques.

* * *

One Saturday night in early June, we went to the dance on Hastings pier to calm our nerves before pre-baiting the Spoon on the snide. Only a week to go now. The Glitter Band came on without Gary and we all booed. Me and Mark had picked up a couple of birds. His had a scab on her lip, mine a pout. We tried to get them behind the curtain but they preferred the Glitters. In the interval, I jockeyed mine outside, I can't remember her name. A dogfish in a black raincoat, floral frock with nylon flowers growing off it. I wore the Invalidity Benefit clothing allowance gear: sale-price, grey velvet jacket, the landing-net flares, tank top, pink nylon shirt. I didn't even have a pen on me. I'd started staring out of bus windows with my mouth open, singing pop songs in my head, like 'Moonlighting' by Leo Sayer, working out the payments due on the one Tony Fordham ten-foot carp rod and Mitchell 410 I'd signed for on the never-never with Bennetts of Sheffield. I couldn't remember the last book I'd read, but it was probably the *Angler's Mail Annual*. The pout kept saying *nah* every time I frisked her over. In the end we just went to the back of the pier, right round the side near the sea anglers. The odd whiting was coming up the side, a flounder, two dabs on a newspaper. The Tilley lamps burned bright, the multipliers were clicking and the sea bells ringing. Christ, they were happy anglers. The tide was whelking the pier legs and the air was half in summer now. It was like I'd just come-to in a parable, gained sudden consciousness before going under for the last time. I knew the lost creature I'd become, recognised the corrupted pastime that specimen fishing was, before I'd even begun it. I couldn't see a way through the dishonest use I'd lent my intelligence to. I promised to resist, revive, read again, write that novel set in a psychiatric hospital, go chub fishing on small streams, get a job. But right now I had to get this closed season sublimation thing over with. Everything else could start tomorrow, after I'd really caught a carp.

There were loads of coarse anglers out that night, hand-lining their eels over the side of the pier, making perch-like yanks at pairs of tights. A bouncer was zipping round with a torch, rounding us up, telling us to get back in the disco. The pier was dangerous and out of bounds except to anglers. He caught me in his beam. I'd been pulling myself with the pouting's hand. I said I was an angler.

'I can see that,' the bouncer said. 'There's fish all down yer trousiz.'

After the dance we went pre-baiting up the Spoon. Pre-baiting was banned, the reservoir was locked and behind a ten-foot security fence. Mark had been buying craft-built sausages from a master butcher. Three pounds at a time, three times a week. He fried them up in his stepmother's kitchen, the best sausages you ever saw, just to chuck in the Spoon. They cost all his dole. He'd chopped them into four and bagged them up before the dance, then gone to see the Glitter Band holding a carrier bag of cold sausages. I was starving hungry. The trouble was that Mark always took a taxi up the Spoon and expected me to split his fares, for putting me up and feeding me. He was excited that night, more than before.

'Just a week to go, moosh. This time next week, I'll 'ave the first double in the sack. Can't go wrong with this bait.'

We walked round the perimeter in the pitch dark, chucking Dewhurst's finest porkers over the fence, waiting till we heard the rusky plosh. He gave me half of them, but it was so dark I ate mine and threw pebbles instead.

THIRTEEN

FARMER RUMMERY HAD a glass eye and a one-acre pond called
Silverden on the edge of his land. I'd been at school with his son
Guy. Farm skin, the colour of a clay pot. Born with the tractor oil in
his blood, he'd been famous for his cheese-and-onion farts in maths.
The Rummerys were fruit farmers. I'd earned some spending money
there myself, so we weren't enemies. That didn't stop his dogs tearing
me apart when I'd knocked on their door earlier in the close season. I'd
been set to launch a take-over bid for Silverden Pond, on behalf of the
specimen group.

Silverden had always been free fishing. On childhood's map, just a
fourpenny bus ride from Hawkhurst and a long walk up the lane. The
fishing bank was well scuffed, the dirt worn to below the tree roots.
There were two real swims, one gap in the bushes, and a few casting
holes in the jungle where the pond narrowed into swamp. Behind you,
the rutted track on the edge of a raspberry field. Opposite, a cottage
lawn sloped down to reeds, out of bounds and strictly private.

It was popular with locals and holidaymakers, even if you never saw
anyone up there. There were plenty of rudd, roach, tench, perch, till the
big perch kill, suspected eels and the usual pike rumour. But my sights
were on a gang of tough carp, the wildie bunch, seen but never caught.
My one motive for annexing Silverden was simple and selfish – to raise
my level of respect in the specimen group.

If they hadn't yet seen me fishing, they'd seen enough to guess that I hailed from the wrong section of the *Angler's Mail*. By pulling off a deal with Rummery, I could buy some time, or grace. From June 16th, I would watch Mark on the Spoon like a spy, then go up Silverden, apply the formula, and catch those carp for the group's Hall of Fame. Mark had an empty photo-flip ready and waiting. Rummery signed my typed agreement, adding two clauses: we couldn't stock it, or 'monkey with it'. No money changed hands, just a bottle of whisky which put a beam in his glass eye. I was vague about management. Maybe he thought we'd keep the gypsies off his plums. Silverden would stay free fishing for all-comers and the specimen group would, well, run it. I didn't know how. We banned night fishing, except for ourselves. Perhaps we'd have overnight group fish-ins. Collect rubbish, keep the peace. Don would hand out the free tickets at our front door. It was, when scrutinised, a white elephant. We could have fished it for free anyway, day or night. Now we were responsible for the state of the place and the behaviour of everyone who fished it.

Nevertheless, the committee failed to spot the flaw and were duly impressed. I was slapped on the back. Mark was a painter and decorator by trade, so he painted a sign. A pompous sign, the wrong side of rural diplomacy. One afternoon we went up there to nail it on the tree. PRIVATE FISHING. NO NIGHT FISHING. NO LITTER. A week later we found the sign floating in the shallows down the other end.

In Hastings, rival specimen gangs without blue membership cards were sneering about us; casual groups who had fished side by side without too much animosity in the past. Declaring yourself a specimen group with ninety-five spare cards was arrogance, a tasteless flaunting of egos in disarray. There was sniping and verbal skirmish, stabs in the back and propaganda. Opening-night blanks were now out of the question.

Mark stepped up his furtive pre-baiting in the final week to give himself an edge but was seen by a rival carper, Bumble, another sneak pre-baiter who lived behind the Spoon. A jealous Marxist, he reported Mark to the club committee, twelve maggot sprinklers who banned everything but the bomb. A ban against Mark was predicted. Royston had to be restrained. Mark went to a solicitor and threatened both club and informant with court action. The committee postponed their meeting so Mark would be able fish the opening week. But the anti-carp movement was now under way. My reluctance to enter such a knowledgeable skirmish made me revise my opening-day plans.

The carp gear came mail order with two days to go. One red, hollow-fibreglass compound taper, ten feet of tranquillity, the Tony Fordham carp rod. My second rod was brown, anonymous, ten feet of floppy generic hollow glass, Royston's spare, a cast-off, his old floating-crust rod. Two Mitchell 410s hung off the bottom. My days as a bread-paste virgin were drawing to a close. The only trouble was, I hadn't found a substitute bait. My finances had been strangled by this equipment and the close-season pecking order. I couldn't afford even a pound of Mark's bangers. This was surely a fussy detail. What was important here was image and sales technique. The *pose*. The look of the warrior's camp, the awe it would inspire in passers-by and schoolboys, fruit pickers and maybe the carp. But, most of all, narcissistic me. I decided on Silverden as the venue at which to unveil my coming to power, to practise it unwitnessed, free of knowing scorn.

I made a mock-up of the scene in the garden, a rehearsal in the June sun among the daisies and the Sunday mow. Mark had shown me pictures of the parallel world, the one in which you used a spirit level to get your two rods exactly parallel, equidistant, ring-to-ring perfect. By teatime I was confident that the denizens of Silverden would have seen nothing so beautiful or compelling. I left everything in the garden till the sun set and the carp started to jump along the front hedge. In the glow off the streetlamp, the new rod didn't quite look right. I'd even rigged them up and tended the lines. Maybe a cat had run off next door with the line as there was a right-hand curve. But the fake bait was where I had left it, nestling at the bottom of the hedge. The sun had warped my new rod, put a curse on it, a nice permanent starboard set. I could have howled well into the night. Every effort to straighten it out failed. I had a freak rod and it was too late to send it back.

It was the story of my life. Back at college, if you'd wanted to be a freak, you had to have long sideburns. One was all right and reached my earlobe, but the other was mostly fluff and curled wisps. I used to sticky tape it to my face every night at bedtime, then lay on it. In the morning I would unpeel the tape and for the moment this sideboard matched the good one, until I'd set off for the bus stop. In the cold morning air it just curled up again. Now my rods were like my sideboards.

My plan to fish alone and unseen suffered similar last-minute curvature. The specimen group sensed I needed vetting. Put bluntly, they anticipated a lie. Alan was unexpectedly free and volunteered to keep me company at Silverden, to see if those tench I had caught when I was fourteen were now plump oldies. On the evening of June 15th Alan picked me up from All Saints with a smirk as bent as my rod. In the car he said:

'What bait you on then, Dex?'

'I've made up some specials,' I said.

He almost vomited through effort to stifle laughter. Unable to remain silent, I said *Don't ask me about my bait.* I counted on the law of the times preventing him from seeing it and really vomiting. In those days bait talk cost lives. All baits were secret, all ingredients rumours, or 'specials'. Even if you shared the cost, you didn't necessarily share identity of a bait. Mark's sausages were top secret, on pain of total ostracising. My own path to bait enlightenment was obstructed by personality and by obdurate parsimony. I decided on a cheap 'special'. I'd read about PYM but misunderstood the science. Anyone could knock some up with bran and brewer's yeast and some home-made breadcrumb from a stale loaf, surely? The result was a plastic bucket full of patio filler, wall plug comedy bait. I moulded a dozen billiard balls of this at the pond then sat and twiddled my thumbs.

Predictably, that evening was forgettable, but not by me. Unforgettable was our tremulous grasp of comradeship and total lack of angling quintessence. Alan was a precision angler. He had come to terms with his ambition, balanced it against the pleasure of catching fish. He had opted to remain an all-rounder, which excluded carp, or, in other words, anxiety. He rigged up in a faultlessly neat pitch, his critically balanced floats, hair-trigger efficiency, all his tackle cleaned, oiled and essential. Calm and quiet, he sat on his blue Argos bed chair and read the paper in a tweed hat, patiently awaiting midnight. Maybe in retrospect it was a bit boy scout, Mac in the shed. His black, thick-rimmed spectacles and flat expression lent him an air of Harry Worth raised in Meccano World while reading *Caravan Weekly*. But I learned some of the rules that day, just by imitation. Simple stealth in action. You whisper at the waterside. You tiptoe, slow motion, tie your hooks against the moon, no torches. You light your fag behind a tree in cupped hands, kneeling with your back to the water. Unforgettable habits.

In contrast to Alan's grace in the field, I was a bundle of undeflated pride. For Alan, Silverden was a country pond where he intended to relax and go fishing. For me, it was a bull ring where I would flog a red rag at my adolescent inferiority. Where I would waste the chance to be an honest apprentice or pleasant company and end up mauled. Most nineteen-years-olds should not be out fishing at all. They should be talking it off in a boasting park. Mine was coward's talk. You know the sort: *I'm gonna do that, I'm gonna do this, and I've got the bait to do it with.* Alan wasn't fooled. If he'd thought he was in the company of an angler, he would have shared his own doubts too. He was a troubled man, but what use is the crude ego next door to a troubled man. Short of asking me if I was thinking of casting in before midnight, the conversation had no motivation. When trying to save the day by hinting that my bucket of 'specials' was as good as Mark's bangers, Alan's blank embarrassed mask finally got through to me. The minute he was back in Hastings he'd be curling up on the floor in a fit as he told Mark and Royston. If only we'd had the intelligence to say: look, let's be honest about this, the rest doesn't matter.

We were both set up well before dark fell. It's a long wait till midnight when one of you isn't right in the head. Perhaps with a cup of tea Alan might treat me as human, so I set about brewing up. I had a Camping Gaz stove I'd not tried out yet. My knowledge of properly equipped night fishing was limited to the dancing float on black ponds, or eel fishing with latch-key kids on the Medway beside a blazing bonfire for heat and light. As I screwed the Camping Gaz canister on to the burner, the hole pierced. My hesitation allowed some gas to spurt out under pressure. In the panic it became a fountain of freezing liquid gas. Fearing explosion, I dunked the canister in the marginal water. It shot off under velocity across the pond, leaving a jet stream, a horror film of frozen anti-angling gas. It settled in the middle of Alan's swim to a steady, declining spin.

Alan was standing behind me now. As liberated as the gas canister. All that pent up mirth spurting out in a string of cold jokes he'd been saving up to tell Mark. His particular skill was sarcasm. It was as critically balanced as his floats. Every detail of my set-up now came under crushing examination, from the 'swing tip' on my new carp rod to the flower pots on the ground under the reel. He said it was like going fishing with Bill and Ben, Charlie Drake and Donald Duck. Then he told me I was a pillock and walked off, back to his *Caravan Weekly*.

We both blanked. Only the disillusion with Silverden was mutual. In the morning, under a grey, windless sky, the water had an unyielding sheen of dead crust where nothing moved. The gas canister marked the spot. Alan's two floats were like photographs pinned on the water. He packed up at ten and left me to dream. Every time I reeled in one of my free-lined specials, I found a stinking black ball of effervescing cake, coated in silt and twigs. Dozens of emergency casts failed to salvage the canister. It was visible as the only litter in scum-corner all season.

By August, Mark had caught ten doubles and his first twenty-pounder. He was rapidly expanding the group Hall of Fame into a one-man cult. Alan had to take a job in Saudi as a matter of urgency. I kept busy by painting everything black. Actual angling techniques were refined in the garden or beside carp-less ponds. I fished the Spoon just once. By then I felt ready, Mark's every carp-wards gesture had burned onto my soul. His free-lined sausages on the end of my line, size 8 Au Lion d'Or hooks buried within, cast into the margins at the foot of the concrete slope. It was mid-August. At 2 a.m., a storm came off the sea, the wind blowing trees over. You could hear nothing but roaring and thunder. My rods were way down the incline. Somehow the sound of my alarm came through. The red light was on. The buzzer sounded like a whistling kettle in a house across the fields. It took me that long to get to it. By then the silver paper bite indicator had wedged firmly in the butt ring. The rod had dragged along the concrete and put a fighting scratch down the reel. The fish had gone.

I was shaken to the core. My first ever run. A great carp digging the rod out and throwing it on the concrete. I could do it, after all. No one else had a run that night. No one else believed me, because they hadn't seen it. They were like that about everything. I was asking myself frequently how I could stop being here. But the run left me too shaken, too in awe of this unseen thing. It finally taught me what I needed to know in the first place.

Then Royston stopped fishing for a life of crime. With Alan in Saudi, Royston's brother-in-law moved in to lodge with Alan's wife, Mary, who needed the cash. Some snoop caught them screwing on a Li-lo in the front room. They eloped together when word went up and Royston threatened to kill them both. He spent weeks driving round Hastings like a vigilante.

'Alan's family. I'm gonna kill the bastard.'

Someone said they were sleeping in the car, kid and all. Mary was too afraid to go back to the house, even to get her stuff. Royston found them parked up in a lay-by and rammed the driver's side doing thirty. Then chucked a breeze block through the windscreen. It put the bloke in hospital. Royston got three months suspended, a big fine and a driving ban.

Mark said I should try sweetcorn up Silverden. I bought two cans and scattered them round the margins. The next day I turned up for a five-day session. It was late August. I set up in perfect carp-night weather, a sultry evening, the smell of mown grass. I opened the first tin of sweetcorn. It was baby food, crushed, cream of Jolly Green Giant sick. I hadn't read the labels properly, being new to this game. I'd bought half a dozen. At least one was a tin of kernels. I had to eek them out for hook bait, and ground bait with the sick.

I was sitting propped against the tree at midnight, chain smoking roll-ups. The next second it was like the waters broke. The buzzer screeched to a blistering run, the silver paper staying up in the butt ring till I clicked over the bail arm and struck. This time it worked. The rod bent in joy for the first time. Line smoked off the spool, the fish halfway up the cottage lawn opposite. The splash rocking the pond like an earthquake. I expected the people in the cottage to dash outside, screaming on to the lawn in their nighties. A 3lb wild carp can do all of that.

Mark would never believe me. Even this tiny fish, by his standards. The rule was photographic evidence. My instamatic camera had no flash. I'd had it since I was ten, free with a couple of Kellogg's coupons. I retained the fish in a hessian coal sack till morning. At sunrise it was dead. It had only been in six inches of water. I violated it with a photograph, just so I could save face and Mark could put it in the records. I should have got three months and a fishing ban for that. I never sacked a fish again.

Specimen hunting needed a perpetual fountain of money. That and ruthless self-delusion. Fish and chips, the bus fares, the one-armed bandits on the pier, the pasties, taxis, angling mags, fags and papers, memberships and that fiver I always seemed to owe Mark when my nine-quid benefit was cashed. So by winter we had all drifted into regular work. The specimen hunting became winter chubbing at weekends. I had come full circle now, back on the Rother chub where I'd started. The four-pounders came. Each fish began to have its own innocence once more, instead of a commodity to barter against local fame. Relieved of the tyranny of the carp, I started to become an angler, but maybe too late.

In November I went to work in the village builder's merchants in Santer's yard. I dumped the flares and wore a cloth cap and nine-hole leather boots now. Every Sunday I went to the pictures with my cousin from Gravesend. We met halfway, in Maidstone. I always had to leave the film ten minutes before the end so she could get her train, and I could catch the bus. I still don't know how *One Flew Over the Cuckoo's Nest* or any of those films ended. But not knowing the end is a way of keeping things open. Specimen hunting seemed like slamming the door shut, narrowing life down to a predictable set of targets, the ambitions of the pack. In rebellion, at last, I began to write that novel, somehow, sitting on the gas fire at work behind the trade counter at 7.30 in the morning, writing it in an old beige war issue Civil Service notebook.

Just as it ceased to matter, I emerged a better angler for this apprenticeship with Mark, Alan and Royston. It lasted a second season; I even caught some carp. It's probably true to say they taught me all I knew at the time. And by default I became a better human, and not in relief to them, but in relation to the qualities they possessed. They were supreme anglers. If I had been either, the need for their kennel mentality would not have arisen. For at least twenty years after, when tying a knot, I would still murmur, as a ritual echo of one of Royston's own dictums: *Five turns and one for luck, as Royston used to say.* Every time I cast, I mimic Mark's perfect eye, his soft style, something you could only learn in the days when baits were free-lined. And as for Alan, I hope I've embodied his calm precision, his love of just being out there fishing, and a house-proud efficiency in the swim. The pride-of-place memory, oddly enough, goes to Royston, who really was a thug, the wildie in the bunch, the most out of control.

We're on the cliff tops along Fairlight at sunrise. There's a sea mist turning custard-yellow and the grass is soaked in dew. We've clambered up from the Spoon a mile away, where Royston kicked me awake at 5 a.m. and said *Come on, moosh, git yer crust rod and come with me.* We've a rod each, a bag of crust, a packet of hooks and a landing net between us. Way down below us is the sea, a guessed-at sound, but the mist begins to part as a breeze wipes it away. The pond is a thousand years old, a hole in the mist, round and less than half an acre, reed-lined and black and dead, dead still. We stand and watch, the blunt noses of torpedoes rubbing through the reeds or sucking down moths. Wild carp, real medieval fish which conquered Hastings in 1066, all golden-green doubloons and shielded up to defend their sanctum, black knights on a cliff top. The swoosh of our crust rods was like arrows at dawn. We'd somehow slipped through that other stupid business going on right then down at the Spoon. We'd come to some agreement with the world. Even if we knew it couldn't last, that we were fishing on the edge of tomorrow, nothing else mattered but that crust on the water and those unyielding wild fish.

FOURTEEN

F ATHER GRIMES WAS WINDING up the end-of-term staff-meeting with his usual pious sarcasm, when a stolen police Land Rover, *Gift of the EEC*, drew up and parked under the school flagpole. It was mid-afternoon. A soldier swaggered over, chewing gum, waving a pistol and petting his greasy mirror shades. The tassels on his fake braid swung like a stripper's.

'Who the devil are you?' Grimes bawled.

'I am Sergeant Benson. I am in charge now.'

Namasagali school was half boot camp, half co-educational Catholic mission in an up-country swamp beside the Victoria Nile. Cut off in the rains, there was no paved road, just thirteen miles of rut and red murrum to a dead end. Jim and I were expat teachers who shared a brooding bungalow on the edge of the school compound. Dilapidation, scrub-jungle, the River Nile running through it. It was here they shot the trailer for *The African Queen*. An abandoned trading post, once a cotton-loading railhead on the old Jinja line.

Benson's men came in the back of a pea-green Tata truck. Its last owner was lying dead two miles down the track. Hungry soldiers with the pox, torn fatigues, white raincoats with glass buttons nicked off missionary women.

'Operations,' Benson said. 'We are looking into bandits.'

It was Uganda, 1980, the same old road to a killing, an anti-bandit sweep through the bush. On paper, the rounding up of guerrilla sympathisers and political troublemakers. In truth they were unpaid, out looting instead of in barracks where they belonged. And, worse still, they should have been under a proper officer, not this Benson masquerading as Idi Amin.

Luckily the school compound was deserted. Half the nine hundred pupils were teenage girls. They'd been packed into old Leyland buses and shipped out for the Easter break the day before. Two hundred had walked home barefoot through the bush. The soldiers bunked down in the dormitories. Grimes and Zonnerveldt, the Dutch bursar, piked-off in a Jeep next morning, heading for the bishop's mission at Jinja. Smuggled beer and telly, safe beds, waited on by nuns. This left me and Jim alone with nothing to eat.

Till then we'd lived on fish and mashed green bananas called *matoke*. We bought our tilapia and Nile perch off the fishermen who trolled the mile-wide basin morning and evening in dug-out mahogany punts. They cycled their catches into the village, 100lb perch over their shoulders, tails dragging in the dust. Strings of tilapia like onions dangling off the handlebars.

School rations were staples, distributed to the twenty teachers by the bursar once a month. Rice, sugar, tea. Sometimes potatoes or flour, oil, and tobacco. We bartered the sugar and spuds with the African teachers who used them to brew moonshine and beer. In the village we might be lucky and find onions, sweet bananas or groundnuts spread on a dirty rag by an old woman. Other times we'd pay a runner boy to go round the bush villages and buy eggs. He would run twenty miles and come back with two eggs, unbroken in a brown paper bag.

Money was meaningless, Uganda shillings worthless. Fat bog rolls of filthy notes for a plate of food. A week's wages for a box of matches. Cigarettes were fifty dollars each. But Benson's arrival emptied the village. Everyone fled into the bush. Even the onion woman. The fishermen hid their punts or rowed across to the other side and stayed there. The runner boy ran. The milkman was arrested and tortured in a lock-up within earshot the first night. And as soon as dark fell, the shooting began. On the second night a soldier fired rocket grenades blindly into the river. One skimmed the trees in our garden. Me and Jim sat up half the night planning our survival. There was only one way to protein: I would have to go fishing.

The problem was our complete lack of tackle. Idi Amin had fled to Libya the year before and the Tanzanian liberators had just withdrawn, leaving Uganda with empty shops and a war debt. The whole country was broke and derelict. Even the animals had run into Rwanda or Tanzania. The last white rhino had been knowingly shot for an army barbeque. President Obote's ministers were already looting the treasury of World Bank and EEC funds. His army was out looting the villages and robbing travellers like highwaymen. Even Museveni had begun his guerrilla campaign with factional in-fighting.

All you could buy in a Ugandan shop was a jar of Petroleum Jelly, a packet of stale tea and a Chinese razor blade. Indispensable items in any angler's tropical kit, of course. Jim, who'd never fished, drew the short straw; he must journey to Kenya with the last of our foreign exchange, about twenty dollars in pocket money. I gave him a simple list. A hundred yards of 6lb nylon mono, packets of hooks sizes 4, 6, 8 and 10. The rest we'd have to improvise. 'Oh, and have a drink on me while you're there, Jim,' I said, instantly regretting the suggestion.

Jim was a miner's son from Clipston, a Nottinghamshire pit village near Mansfield, where the women were allowed in the pub only on dominoes night, where the sons of Lawrence staggered home at closing time, half-mauled by eight pints and a chip butty, ready to fight their fathers bare knuckled with a poker. Jim's father had been a lay preacher in a strict chapel sect, the most hated man in the village. He turned Jim into a Marxist atheist poet, a leg-chopping full-back, smokes at half-time, rat-arsed after the game, not the most lyrical of combinations. But for all this Jim was a trooper, the one you'd choose if you were down to two men.

On fishing-tackle day, I rose before dawn after another sleepless night on murder watch. I lit the charcoal, took Jim some coffee. He was still out cold so I knocked him awake and told him the coast was clear. The thing about Jim was his knack of blocking out the anxiety through visceral procedure. The pit-works of his body always came first. We were both twenty-four. I smoked as many as Jim, but could still do ninety minutes with the school First XI. Jim was on his knees after ten. Every morning, his routine was like a flight check in a Lancaster bomber, flicking the switches, creaking the flaps, opening the bomb bay. Only when he was certain he'd live another day did he open his eyes and take off.

I can't deny my Sunday school sniffing at Jim's animal disregard. The conversations with his 'guts', licking his plate, taking his dentures out and sucking the food off, the ringmaster farts and seismic belching. The bogies and dandruff, the ball-scratching, jigger-hatching lice-filled beard, mongering lazy-eye piles, every chromosome and particle of him was on display, in class, in staff-meetings, at supper, under fire, at the going down of the sun.

Today I counted on it. Any different and we might very well die. He blew his throat inside out, ran his hand over the concrete floor in the dark, feeling for his false teeth, somewhere there among the dropped ash, pinched nub ends, splashed coffee. A game Jim relished. Every night the cockroaches formed a seething dome over his teeth, picking them clean and shiny. He struck a match. The candle stub spat bad wax. His toothpicks scuttled away under the wainscot.

'Blood and sand, youth,' he said.

'You still up for this?'

A roaring yawn echoed around the bare room.

'Wild horthith, youth.'

He belched and brayed his way upright, scuffed along the unswept veranda in car-tyre flip-flops. The biggest dog-end off the floor poked from his mouth and lit off the candle stub. A *Guardian Weekly* in his other hand, teeth in his pocket. The *Guardian Weekly* was a subscription digest of the London *Guardian*, *Le Monde*, and *The Washington Post*. It was printed on airmail paper. Jim read it sheet by sheet. I read the book reviews, did the cryptic crossword, thumbed through for anything on Uganda, then we cut it up for cigarette and toilet paper. The pot-holed infrastructure meant it arrived five issues at a time in the school PO box thirty miles away in the bush.

Jim stood in the bog doorway, running the candle stub round the corners for snakes. We always did this, after the morning he'd parked his bare arse on a black mamba. The mamba was already dead. It had probably crawled out the toilet, which wasn't plumbed to a water supply. The soil pipe went straight down the garden and into the River Nile. We flushed our muck with a bucket of Nile and didn't wonder much what lived in the pipe or where the muck ended up. I left him straining and set off to make sure the lorry owner was still alive and had diesel. Jim was singing: *Gone fithin' thaid the thign upon the door...*

We did everything in the river except fish it. Washed in it, fetched it in buckets to boil and drink and flush. By imaginative oversight I'd come to Africa without any fishing tackle. I didn't actually own any. I'd sold it in 1977 to fund estrangement from disillusion and to slip behind the Iron Curtain.

Anna was a Polish au pair I'd met at the Zippy Bar in Tunbridge Wells in 1974. She'd said she was looking for a husband so she could 'get visa and go to United States'. Pretty soon I became, in her words, 'loneliest person' she knew. She was lonely too, hated her job and loathed the English. She smoked Marlboro like a slut with a mop and soon found a job as a chamber maid in one of those big residential hotels in London Road. She visited me in hospital, not because she liked me, she said, but because the patients' library was full of Polish books and it was the only place she could find any. The long-stay wards were full of Poles dumped there after the war. A couple of times we'd gone to her room down in the basement. She brought me tea from the kitchens, we talked about whatever she was reading. Then once, in my lonely clothes, I did a striptease which sort of baffled both of us but she found it amusing. She didn't seem interested in sex but she gave me a hand-shandy, then I put my clothes on and got the bus back to Hawkhurst.

She wasn't pretty. She had a broken nose, hairy legs, but full lips, which might have been useful sucking venom from a snake bite or vice versa. You wouldn't know till it happened. One day she said she wanted to lose her virginity and she'd chosen me instead of Ricardo, the Colombian waiter. On the way to her room she borrowed a Johnny off Ricardo. We swigged some vodka. The rest was dry fumbling without conviction on either side. Anna said *All right, stop, is enough, go, get your bus, leave me alone.*

That night the phone rang, at 2.30 a.m. It wouldn't stop ringing. The phone was at the bottom of the landing stairs, magnified by a workshop bell Mac had rigged up in the kitchen. I opened my bedroom door and found Don on the landing in the midst of her Mogadon nightmare. *You've done it this time,* she said, picking up the phone.

'Who's that?! What yer ringing 'im now for? Don't you know what time it is?'

'Why did you do it?' Anna shouted. 'Why, why, why? Tell me, you pig. You are pig with brain, you are sex maniac, and your mother is common woman.'

'I can't talk now,' I said. 'It's the middle of the night. You've woken my parents.'

'I don't care for bloody parents. Why did you do it?'

'Why did you ask me? You asked me.'

'You didn't have to do it. I am ashamed. I'm Catholic girl from Nowa Huta.'

She went back to Nowa Huta. Four years later in December 1977, aged twenty-one, I was on a train rattling through East Germany at night with a suitcase full of Tampax, a spermicide applicator, ten Pink Floyd albums to sell on the black market, a shop-soiled wedding dress for a fiver, and a cheap band of gold from Ratner's crap in Oxford Street.

I'd sold the rods to pay the bride price. The ease of the betrayal had shocked me. By Christmas Eve I was sitting in Anna's parents' bath tub in the steel town of Nowa Huta. The Christmas dinner was swimming between my legs: two mid-double mirror carp. They'd been taken out of the bath and put in buckets for my convenience. They'd leapt for it, of course, upending their buckets and toppling back into my bath. They were both bigger than anything I'd ever caught on those silly carp rods. Outside it was minus 21. The lesson learned was a simple but messy one, and the marriage was shorter than a thirty-day eel session.

I'd gone to Africa to escape Anna and to become a man. I've no compunction saying so. Not having a pater who could have packed the n'er do well off to join the colonial police, I'd had to forge a Middlesex Polytechnic Cultural Studies degree and wander there myself. A year in the Sudan teaching market boys 'Androcles and the Lion', drifting south over the Ugandan border, me and Jim, two rough poets making their way down the Nile.

At Namasagali, the river heaved with treble-figure perch. The only carp rod and Mitchell 300 in Uganda belonged to my head of English, a Yorkshireman who lived at the other end of the compound. As soon as I'd heard this, I went tearing up there, excited about fishing again. Instead of the genial ruddy-faced clerk, I found a bush-stiff in his garden, hoeing rock-hard dirt barefoot, thick black beard and leather face. An expat gone native, he'd taken an illiterate wife from the local Busoga tribe. He refused to speak English, jabbering Swahili in my face. When I mentioned his fishing rod, he switched to native Yorkshire.

'Get bloody lost and don't bother me again.'

'Have you caught much with it?'

'I've had eighty-pounders up at Murchison Falls.'

'What about here?'

'Can't be bothered. Haven't used it for five years.'

'Just lend it to me once, then. I'm an angler.'

'Get lost. A Mitchell 300 isn't a toy, you know.'

The lorry was fired up, smoking, knocking and ready to go. I shook hands with the driver and told him Mr Jim was coming. I found Jim still on the veranda steps, dressed, as always, in a ragged white Sudanese *aragi,* like the *waleds,* the turn-boys in bus parks. He had ten minutes so we lingered a moment. We reckoned he might make Busia that day if he was lucky. He tore some airmail paper into thin strips to make smokes on the journey. Fresh fag from the pouch, bathed his lungs, hawked up on to the path. We watched the mist lift, heard the trees drip, the swamp hiss with rising day, the echoes of swirling fish in the river basin. A pale sun rose against the mist as fish-eagles swooped into the bright. It was time. We set off through a compound of deserted houses and I wondered if I'd ever see him again. Jim climbed aboard and I waved and shouted *Good luck* as he set off to find us a fishing-tackle *duka* in Kenya.

I had three days' supply of mouldy food and a pouch of Dutch

Drum tobacco. Jim's reward at the border would be eggs, chips and Peptang sauce. I feared his plan was to get rat-arsed in a native dive with a Johnny Walker girl in his iron bed for a night. He was going on leave, after all.

That night they tortured Wilson, one of the school *askari*, a watchman. I sat in the dark listening to giant perch crashing in the long glide below the old crane. Convinced I could see the silhouette of a soldier with a rocket launcher crouched beyond the veranda mesh, I stared at him for hours. It was just a bush. I hadn't night-fished for so long. One night at Delmonden I'd been convinced another angler was fishing opposite. I saw his silhouette, heard him cast, the bail arm on his reel click over, his fart, the sweetcorn he scattered round his bait. The more I stared through the dark, the more I saw him. I was glad of the company. In the morning he was just a tree stump, a bush, the ringing in my ears.

Wilson's screams were like the bobcats who sometimes ate their prey in front of the house. Wilson had no mouth, his one tooth stuck out from his nose. By day he sat weaving on his rush mat under a *mvule* tree, astride swollen bollocks arranged like coconuts outside his shorts. He'd pause from his basket-weaving to greet you by holding up his old tin by the string handle, sipping at the fresh milk which frothed down his chin, his baskets arranged beside him.

Next day Tinka was gone from his command post in the school radio room. Now we were effectively cut off. I didn't know the call sign, and there was no electricity now, and no fuel for the generator. The Ugandan flag hung limp over the assembly square with its white stone border. The soldiers were away in the bush. The boys' dormitories were like vandalised empty warehouses. Long dilapidated rows, rusted iron bunks like they'd been dragged out of the river. Dogs barked, cocks crowed. Young girls appeared from the forest paths with buckets on their heads. I ducked under the school barrier into the village street. The *askari* sprang from his bench, pulling the bush hat elastic under his chin. No, he said, the soldiers had not gone. They were sleeping somewhere. They were coming back. *They want fish, but the fishermen are hiding.*

Jim was back in four days. I was on the veranda drinking black tea and smoking a *Guardian Weekly* when he appeared, slapping the dank corners of his travel bag for the fishing hooks. The bag was a Sudanese camel's gut with a strap. It stank like a camel's gut too, shanks of desiccated meat still welded to it.

'I know I had 'em, youth. Mustad 'ooks.'

He looked rough but triumphant. He'd survived the roadblocks, the UPC Youth Wingers looting passengers, the triple-articulated petrol tankers from Burundi. These freewheeled down long sharp hills to save diesel and collided with the Peugeot 504s. Bush taxis Jim would have taken, stuffed with up to twenty passengers freewheeling down the other side to save petrol. The fires would burn for days. In fact he'd made the Kenyan border at sunset on the first day, then dived straight into a bar. Rat-arsed with a tart, according to plan. He's still alive today and not dead of AIDS because he remembered his task, passed out with brewer's droop, then woke to find himself alone. The dollars were still down his trousers, hook, line and sinker on his conscience.

Rods and bait were the next project. Jim was a gardener from the cradle, the sort of bloke who'll double dig for victory. He'd even cleared a patch of scrub out front and planted beans, which were now small green shoots awaiting rain. I wondered if he was up for a wormery.

'Worms, youth? No worms in Africa.'

I didn't know this. We rooted in the scrub after insects and grubs. A mamba's nest writhing with worm-sized elver lookalikes had us running for the house. You'd think they'd make a great bait until you realised even a three-inch mamba carries enough venom to kill ten anglers in ten minutes.

Father Grimes had given us a houseboy called Moses, whom he'd trained himself. Me and Jim were anti-colonial commie scum. We said we didn't want Moses, but he came hang-dog from the bush every morning with an egg. He lit the charcoal stove and swept the floor when we weren't looking. He liked Mr Jim, his fart and belching bonhomie. I was more your aloof pith-hat poet. I resented Moses's ghostly walking through walls. When Jim had taken leave, so had Moses, but here he was again, minutes after Mr Jim's return. Moses's mud-hut village was five miles away. The bush telegraph. Moses had braved the soldiers, so I acted graciously. I asked him what the fishermen used as bait. Worms, he said. Jim was sceptical. I gave Moses a rusty tin and told him to fetch some. He came back with a foul-smelling tin of sludge which stirred and popped from occupation. Worm-like creatures from the deep, livid slithering white bacon rinds I'd seen in nightmares. Moses had gathered them from the school latrines. Intestinal worms.

Tackle was as knock-up as the tactics. Two papyrus whips growing by the river to fish the dung-worms for live bait. The other was a stepped-up pole from a custard apple tree. This was to catch a three-course dinner. Jim would join me with a whip, then once the live bait was out he'd light the charcoal, fan the flames and sharpen the filleting knife. Bayer Perlon, size 10 Mustad, bit of crimped tin for a weight and we sat on the old jetty with our dung-worms jigging. Jim was first away with an eight-ounce electric guppy. I was next and landed a sort of lemon-yellow sea-horse with an orange saddle. We thought they'd escaped from the zoo under Amin. I rigged up the bigger pole with a two-inch wrasse from Mars and swung it into the current. It wasn't there ten seconds before the line snapped tight and the battle was on. I told Jim to watch out for soldiers, but he was off to light the charcoal. Quite right too. I swung up a two-pound tilapia. We ate three that night and laughed till bloody sunrise.

Next evening I settled in the same swim on the old loading quay. The rusty crane to my left had a boiler with a plaque, *Made in Birmingham, 1919*. Details of the last load were still chalked up on a broken slate, still in the office with its roof caved in. I sat with my legs dangling down the concrete sides. It looked like rain, so I had an old raincoat half-draped, half-leaning on my back. There were shots in the far distance, the other side of the river. We were used to that now. Some of the soldiers had gone after the fishermen. It was otherwise calm, the air still and heavy. The weird fish weren't biting, the dung-worms had lost what freshness they may have had. I was still too, and this is important to note. I was dead still, even contemplative. I was aware of a light flicking on the arm of my raincoat, still draped over my shoulders. I imagined it to be the grass flicking in the tiny breeze, which stirred now and then, or a winged insect. I sat on, unmoved, while the boomslang, the deadliest snake in East Africa, went up one sleeve, across my back and out the other sleeve. If I'd had a bite on the rod, I would have been dead. If some stupid sea-horse mouth-brooder with my number in orange dots on its brisket had grabbed that shit-worm, I would have struck, and so would the boomslang. Less than three minutes to wish I had given up fishing for good.

I didn't realise it was a snake until it began to emerge from the left sleeve. From sitting dead still, I froze, which is not the same thing to a snake. You send signals down your veins a snake can pick up. And worse are the signals you send yourself. It seemed to hesitate, but kept going. Snake in the grass, tufts between the fissured concrete. And still I didn't move, not even an eye, the corner of which it inhabited a moment, then bisected it cleanly, into the undergrowth. I gave it twenty seconds, then moved my head. There he was, stretched full length and waiting across the path behind me. There was something I didn't like about this. Something Sergeant Benson-like. Did he know I couldn't swim? Something I learned later, something like an idiot I'd avoided, a skill all fishermen should be forced to learn before getting a licence. The number of times I'd nearly fallen in to certain death outweighed all my encounters with snakes. So my choice was jump in the river or wade through the equally snake-infested scrub either side of the path. This yellow-green assassin knew it. The quayside was Plimsoll-line depth, way out of mine. Swimming wasn't safety anyway. The boomslangs hung draped from the riverside papyrus, amphibious by nature. They were at their most active by evening. Once, when standing knee-deep in the river washing my hair, a two-foot black mamba had swum between my legs.

Death came downriver most weeks that year. One weekend, three bodies, two tied with rope and adipose, washed up where the kids dipped. Three S4s on penalty fetching water found the first one. The school court had sentenced them to fetch water and receive ten lashes. They came running back, jibbering about a body in the washing bay. They shouldn't have been near the washing bay. Grimes gave them ten extra penalties, enough for another court appearance. On hearing about the bodies, the African staff had begun packing their suitcases and hiding them among the banana trees. They said the soldiers were on their way downriver. The body was a man who had a cassava factory just this side of the Nalwekomba River. Grimes adjourned court and took me and the school nurse with him. Mr Kintu, the art teacher, insisted on coming. More teachers were hiding their belongings, saying there were two bodies now. Mr Kintu knew the second man. He said it was Elijah from the ginnery in Kasozi. He'd been gone a whole week after running away with four million shillings off his brother-in-law. Chencha, the maths teacher, joined in and said Elijah was alive in Jinja. He began issuing threats, saying the soldiers will want to see everyone's UPC card, the Uganda People's Congress, the President's party. Others said there was no body at all, so then it was witchcraft. A jealous classmate had got the five boys into trouble and made them hallucinate. The teachers all took turns shoving at the bodies with poles, terrorised. Then an argument began. UPC said it was the bandits. Democratic Party teachers said it was UPC Youth Wingers at Owen Falls roadblock killing the passengers. I suggested the Nile perch would have eaten them long before they reached here, that's if they even beat the rapids. They must have been local. They hadn't come far because the fishermen would have dragged them behind their *ngulawa* boats for bait. They did this often, snagging them in a net and towing them for rubber-dubby. God knows how many dinners me and Jim had eaten which might have qualified as cannibal. Grimes had put an end to all debate and said: *Three bodies on a Saturday do not make revolution.*

It was me or the snake. I didn't fancy being bait for the fish I intended to catch. I leapt, I swear, six feet into the air, hit the path and ran the hundred yards in ten seconds. Jim had the charcoal going. Such faith in my angling, such Jesus-like advice at my empty and imaginary creel. His pragmatic refusal to empathise with my lucky escape led merely to *Cast your line on the other side man, where we wash.*

Something seized me, besides certain hunger. I was beginning to understand fishing now. And at night, in the dirty yellow flame of a smoking rag-lamp, I thrashed at the typewriter and a voice which belonged to me was coming through. The words were making sense at last. With the same dawning confidence, I threaded yesterday's tilapia head on to the line, rigged a kind of snood-cum-tropical-paternoster, whipped a cradle to a twelve-foot pole hacked from the fishing-rod tree, and hand-cast it lasso-style into the deep glides beyond our washing spot. The end of the thirty-five yards of Perlon was secured to the butt. The loose portion in between was my 'playing' slack, my fighting drag. I lit a *Guardian Weekly* and sat back. It was all or nothing now, a grand on the outsider. We had the school salt and plenty of smoke. A big perch would feed us till Benson had killed everyone but us and gone home. Jim was beside me when the run came, line hurtling through fingers. I whacked into it as a show of strength, like trying to brain a fly with a broomstick. It stripped my slack like it was spending its winnings, came to the end, hit the knot like a train on a crash barrier and stripped the pole with the skin off my hands. Then the pole disappeared, like a giant float, into the basin, a hundred yards in three seconds, pretty good for a fish, a hundred-pound fish too, as Mr Thatcher would have confirmed. It was all over. End of the line.

'Blood an' sand,' Jim said. 'We're gonna die now, man.'

Our death was Empire Made. Back then, some vestige of fair play still clung to the flagpole at sundown. A battered yellow Audi with diplomatic plates parked under it. Benson had gone, Tinka had crawled from his bush village and radioed through to the British Consulate for help. Pete Roffey was the commercial attaché, an ex-carpet salesman in a Croydon department store. On behalf of Her Majesty the Queen, he asked how we were and handed us a white sliced loaf and a bottle of Greek red wine.

FIFTEEN

THE CANAL HAD A TWILIGHT familiarity. I'd seen it on bedsit tellies, late-night fifties murder films which open with a couple of beatniks sitting on wicker baskets, reeling in a corpse for Inspector Gideon. They always got it wrong in those films, beatniks with a sea rod, fishing the Hackney Regent's Canal. But it was still a murder zone, the local pole-fishers' spittoon, scrap dump, car bodies, human bodies.

Fresh out of Africa, I was lodging round the back of Victoria Park, Hackney, London E9, on the dole, not using that part of the brain which makes intelligent associations. Every day I walked and cycled round Victoria Park Lake, along the River Lea, the Lea Navigation, the Hackney Regent's Canal. These alien, murky Metropolitan slumways with towpaths, derelict wharves and broken factories did not communicate fishing. The wrappers on the park lake, the oil slicks, the bobbing polystyrene, sunken plastic bags, shopping trolleys, battery acid. I viewed the wheezing belly-men with pity, sitting on their boxes, fishing with line as fine as spider web just to fool a slither of detritus. One day I saw a big blind trout twitching through the gunge with a size 1 treble hook in its back.

Bucolic origins had been abandoned, entombed within that country churchyard of youth. Without irony, I dressed like Dick Walker and his gentleman carp fishers had in the 1950s. The sheeny thorn-proof Burton suit from a charity shop, the trilby, stout shoes and short back and sides. All it lacked was the landing net leaning against the tree behind me. The daily walk excluded fish-spotting. The X-ray gaze of the angler had fallen into disrepair eight years back. It gave way instead to the gathering of sordid impressions fit only for the wretched prose I concocted in my digs. But I must have sensed that something was absent, surely? Or at least incomplete in my assessment of these waterways, for it was the water which drew me daily.

I continued to live my daily life as a neutral, just in case that absence revealed itself and needed a place to stay. The loss of angling in life only leads you into listless confusion, compensatory over-production of mediocre theory about life. The time on your hands will not wash off and you save it up till one day you open life's cupboard and it all falls out in a heap, like a load of empty gin bottles. You become easily influenced, but your understanding of the world diminishes. Authority and organisation become enemies, but nothing coherent comes to mind as a replacement. In 1985, we simply blamed Margaret Thatcher for whatever depth of failure we sank to. My indirect demonstration against her was to lead the nocturnal life of a rejected, unpublished novelist. I looked like any Hackney, DHSS, *City Limits*-reading, bike-riding, anti-nuclear, fare-dodging unemployed twenty-nine-year-old with a chip against the cultural norm, harbouring my novel like a hoard of bad coin. Then, one June afternoon, I walked to the lake in Victoria Park in my Dick Walker disguise and I saw *them*. Carp anglers, like a triptych in a holy chapel.

The existential vacuum within was instantly filled. All my instincts and empathies poured from the old dusty suit. The scene was surreal in its awakening. The rods on rod rests were like crutches from Dalí nightmares. The long droop in the lines as they spanned what I could now deduce was shallow water all the way to the island. Nothing had induced me to wonder about its depth before. In floods of recollection I saw every dimple in the cork handles of the rods I owned no more, the ritual of tying the rigs, the mystical arrangement of the sundries in a tackle box, and the one true, vital element I had somehow overlooked: I was an angler, after all, and I wanted to be an angler again. You only lose the fish, not the fishing.

But how or when could I fish again? Why? To be an urban angler meant relinquishing self-conscious neutrality. It meant exposure, class anxiety, double identity. Hackney was the poorest borough in Britain. The yuppies were moving in. Hackney was one-in-three unemployed. The famous-in-waiting squatted the hard-to-lets. Petty criminals lived next door. It was two days queuing at the Social Security to get seen. Public-school buskers and film students had become the slum poets of life-long tenancies after the council advertised tower blocks on a first-come basis. And these people, they were now my friends. It was a borough with an identity crisis and a scoffing resentment of the newcomers with weird hair, whacky ideas and posh accents. At best it was an uneasy truce between drug dealers and Asian shops, dub and punk, white artists and ganja dens, alternative poets and eel-and-pie purveyors, installation galleries, health food co-operatives and pet shops selling pythons and Rottweilers. It was Jacuzzi parlours beside Turkish sweatshops. Temperance hotels opposite bookies. Hackney was a fuck-up with waters to fish.

I carried the stupor all day. It was like regaining your sight, discovering you have something to live for in all this broken glass. Within a week my whole view on the new and crushing concrete world had changed. The three carp anglers had come and gone like a vision. No one knew who they were, and they were never seen fishing there again.

I haunted the waterways with new but conditional vision. Now I saw carp rolling on the park lake. The canal had some lovely eel swims. I imagined myself putting a bait under that collapsed pontoon, and one on the far side by the snagged pallet. I wondered if the banks were too hard for rod rests. Were there tench in the evenings by those reeds? That was a pike. That was a perch chasing fry. Surely there were carp along the Tee. And the belly-men and rockers with sea rods? I would stand and watch them now, spellbound by a waggler rod or the needle float on the end of a pole, recalling an old language I began to use once more.

'Any good, mate?' I'd say.

'Nah, just scratchin', mate,' they'd say.

Mate. That warmed me more than all the semiotics tosh I heard down the Photographers' Gallery or the swish-swash swill on the

Troubadour poetry nights. Yet still I faltered. I would have to demolish the façade, throw back the covers. I wasn't certain how to start, or what needed shifting, or where round these parts you threw your disguise. In the canal, like everyone else, perhaps, where there was always the risk of reeling it back in. Whatever held me aloof was stubborn and officious. Nothing short of orders from on high would raise the barrier. On June 24th 1985, I turned thirty. I never doubted those orders were on their way.

In the grey light of a mid-summer morning, a solitary birthday card arrived. Don's blue biro, addressed with her tongue in her teeth. Pocket fluff on the ballpoint, dents *from us both*. Inside was a fiver flattened in half like an ironed handkerchief ready for school. A fiver was a start, an *Angling Times,* a spool of line, a pair of rod rests. I didn't know. What if it was fading out again? How could I keep it alive? I'd stood by the water, I'd tried the air rod in my room. At the electronic till in the corner shop, I'd heard flashbacks to the old Heron bite alarms ringing in my ears, Mark's voice saying *Hit it, Dex.* I didn't know where, or who, or what I was once more, yet. As June warmed the water, I sat for hours smelling the lake. It was the smell of carp. I breathed it, sucked it deep into my lungs, like I was trying to die of passive angling.

By teatime the light had turned that dead-thumb blue of the fiver, a fresh bruise which promised rain. On the landing outside my room, the pay phone rang in imitation of the card.

'It's me,' the voice said. 'How've yer bin, then?'

'All right.'

'Only all right? Why don't you ever let yer ol' ma know 'ow you are?'

'Well, nothing much happens.'

'No? Nothin' much ever 'appens to me, neether.'

I could tell her mood then. Alone with her one boy, out of earshot from Mac and softening in secret. Red-rimmed eyes, white knuckles gripping a ladies' pocket handkerchief.

'All alone are yer, boy?'

She'd rather I had jelly-mould rabbits on the table, little paper-hatted fishing friends playing blind man's buff.

'Yes yes, quite alone.'

'Got no frenz, then, 'ave yer?'

It would have been easier to say no, but this might've tipped her into lost plenitudes of motherhood, filling to the brim as she was. Now I remembered why I'd started fishing in 1965.

'One or two. Why?'

I knew why. I wished I hadn't said that.

'Oh, I dunno. Just wondered. We ain' got many frenz, neether.'

A life-long sigh, a few seconds till the next as she diddled with the yellow blind.

'Oh, well, yer sister's on 'er 'ollydays. Gone to Wales they 'ave, so we've got Fluffy. Y've not seen Fluffy o' course. Lovely l'il doggy she is. L'il Yorkie. Ever s' nice. Juss like Cindy. Remember Cindy, boy? You there, boy?'

Cindy had been hit by a bus in the beginning of winter, 1965. *That* 1965, my first winter as a boy who goes fishing. I was making a tackle box from plywood. It was teatime. In those days a knock at the front door during teatime made the cream bun congeal in your throat. Turned you to stone. Off goes the telly as Mac's napkin flies across the table. All the family gripe went into his: *Oh Botheration, now who's that?* Mac opened the front door and let the cold under the table, aching round our legs. The voice of Bill Owen from over the road, the bus driver who lived with his old mum.

'Evenin', Mac.'

'Evenin', Bill.'

'Sorry to bother yer, Mac. That your dog up the bus station be any chance? Bin uhm, Fred Chapman like, e's gonna put'er out of 'er misery, you know, with 'is tyre lever if it ain't yawn.'

Don bolted to the shed.

'Oh, father, yer left the blinkin' door open, an' I bet Dexter never shut the gate neither.'

She just made it to the sink. I fingered the masticated bun out of my mouth so I didn't puke in turn. That would be the last time we had cream buns. She ran the tap hard through the rubber nozzle and came in patting her mouth. Mac had the torch out.

'Put yer wellingtons on,' she said.

'I'll take the car.'

'That won't start in this cold and you know it.'

Bill Owen still shuffled in the porch, heels banging against the tin bread box.

'I'll run y'up there, Mac. It were my bus, mate.'

Cindy came home in a cardboard box. The vet pulled two pups out before she died.

'Keep them warm,' he said. 'Feed them with this teat and they'll be right as rain.'

Mac tried his bedside manner out on me first:

'Move yer blessed fishin' tackle out the way.'

He unplugged the money-saving infra-red heat lamp from the bathroom and rigged it up over the puppies, in the shed under the shoe table where I kept the cane rod and its tackle. Next morning before Mac and Don were up, I ran downstairs. All I found were two charred hot-dogs which lay on a smoking blanket.

'DAD. DAD. Y'VE BURNED THE PUPPIZ.'

Mac's feetskin slacked over the cold lino, denture palette clicking.

'Oh fer cryin' out loud. Ow was I t' know the blessid bulb was too hot. It's chilly enough on the bathroom ceiling.'

He unhooked his anorak from a nail, slogged into wellingtons and chose a spade. Don huffed in behind them.

'Right, that's it! No more dogs after this. Not fer love nor money, an' I'm fed up always tripping over this blessed fishin' tackle.'

'Who wazzat?' Don said down the phone.

'Who was what?' I said.

'Juss then. I 'eard someone tawkin' t' yer.'

'No one's talking to me.'

Outside it started raining. The London sky like a lead works. I might have mentioned it, asked if it was raining in Kent. On those still, rust-water ponds. The first tench I caught from Silverden was after the rain lifted on a dull afternoon like this, the float beginning its drunken lurch amid a cloud of tiny bubbles.

'We might go away for a coupla days in August, somewhere.'

'What? It's a bad line,' I said, even though it wasn't.

'I said, we might go away, for a couple of days in August, somewhere nice.'

'What, instead of somewhere horrible,' I said, 'like *we* used to?'

'Now-now, boy.'

But she knew. We shared the same memories. Wherever we went, Mac didn't want fishing rods cluttering up the car and poking him in the neck.

We both said: *Oh well*, several times into, and after, the silences.

'What?'

'Nuffin'.'

The family silence too. A slight crackling on the line, the long distance of crossed voices, two women on a party line in a stream of joyous conversation.

'Well,' I said, 'I shan't be going anywhere.'

'No?'

She didn't sound surprised. I did so little she knew of. The reason I fished through childhood was to create my own world. One where parents didn't trespass. One which kept me outside on rainy days. As a fisherman you belong to no one. And that was suddenly the point. They thought I didn't fish any more, that I belonged to them, that I'd lost interest and sunk into family failure. So I said:

'Just fishing. I'll be going fishing, of course.'

'Oh,' she said. 'Thought you'd given up fishin', boy.'

She made it so accusative, like it was recidivist of me.

It was early evening. The drizzle had probably stopped, because I could smell the barbecues. All the neighbours had them. Yuppies with garden-centre patios and statuettes. They were rigging up the stereo speakers. Don could hear South American panpipes.

'What's goin' on there?'

She didn't like it. I hadn't told her about my party or that I still went fishing. I knew I *would* go fishing now. I was impatient for the call to end. There was planning and dreaming, and fortitude to discover. Knots to tie. Then an ice cream van came down the street, drowning us out with *I love to go a-wandering*. I hadn't heard what she'd said.

'What?'

'What yer mean, what? I said Happy Birf'day.'

'Oh. Yes.'

'Well? Did yer get me card, then?'

'Yes, thanks.'

'It was a nice card,' she said.

'Yes it was.'

'Whass that racket now?' she asked. 'They in your place? They gonna get you in shtook, boy?'

'I'm not having a party, if that's what you think.'

'Whirrrl, if you say so. I believe yer. Yerse, anyway, Piper's got several cards like that, old village scenes and that.'

So here we were at last, at the village crossroads, a point so familiar. If she didn't have village news to impart, I could excuse myself. Say as usual that the bath was running, or the kettle might boil over and extinguish the gas. At this she'd panic, urge me to run in case the house exploded. With her consent I would slam the phone down.

If ever she had news, she hoarded it, dusted it, sliced it reluctantly, threw out the crusts. If she said more than ten words it was like she'd broken a promise.

'Oh well, bedder get back to me ironing, I suppose. Bit of a nuisance, but there we are. Hass t' be done, I'm afraid.'

This was a signal. The uncharacteristic confession. Life-long duty had become a nuisance worthy of remark on my birthday.

'Suppose so,' I said, playing along.

'Yerse, things muss go on, musn't they.'

She was hesitant now, listening out for Mac, making sure he was still outside bleeding his brakes or mowing the lawn. Something had happened down there.

'No news, then. Nothing happened down there.'

I made my appeal sound so hopeless. No question mark in the voice.

'Well, don't rightly know,' she said. 'Might be somming you didn't know about.'

She was taking one last guard, listening for the curdling of mower blades. Or was Mac leaning over the hedge for a chinwag with Doug Cavey?

'No 'arm menshning it now,' she said, 'though yer father might say different.'

There was no point coaxing her. She had to enjoy her indiscretion. She was that one-fag-a-day housewife. One Kit-Kat a week. One gin and lime a month. One perm per quarter, one day-trip on the coach a year, one friend for life.

Whatever I said now she would still pick straws, dither, filter the grit, dust and dust till she could see her reflection in it. Was it nothing? Did it matter? Would Mac hear? Would he know afterwards? Would he come in and catch her? She was taking too long.

'What is it, then? This news.'

I tried to sound so bored.

'Whirl, it weren't nice. Awful for Edna and the boys.'

'What,' I said. 'What's happened?'

It was like waiting for an egg to boil, or a trap to spring. A carp to suck in that floating crust. The stage where every second is too late.

'I didn't tell yer 'cause we're all so shocked.'

'Shocked about what, fer chrissake?'

'Old yer 'orses, boy. Just listen. I'm sorry to say, Doug Cavey died.'

'Oh,' I said. 'What of?'

'Whirl, it was a terrible thing. He took his own, you know. He shot 'imself.'

She said it like she'd lost a bet with herself, like ten to one she'd be telling Doug the bad news about me. But perhaps we knew, him and me, what it was all about before any of them. For once I listened spellbound to Don's voice. The awful truth of Doug's last walk down the front path. Then just as suddenly she pulled up.

'Yer father's juss come in, haha. Gone t' wash 'is hands in the sink. Weather all right in London, is it?'

The conversation was lost. It was her last drag and she was hastily stubbing it out. She'll be caught, words still smoking, flapping the telephone directory like a fan.

'I'd better go, then,' I said.

She couldn't hang up. She'd hung on too long and now Mac would be suspicious. She would brood for weeks and upset everything. It wouldn't matter what she did, Mac would snap and Don would bang the milk pan down.

'D' ya wanna word with yer father?'

'I've got to go,' I said, and I hung up on her.

I walked to the park lake. Hackney was pressed under a flat-iron sky. No one was fishing, the water was still and green, feathers becalmed. A carp rolled by the island. An oily wave spread like a black eye around it, like a wreath on a dead man's front door. I stood looking at the water till it became a blur.

Doug had learned to drive. He took delivery of a new car and that weekend his sons came to visit. The whole family were with him, wife, sons, daughters-in-law, the grandchildren. They went home on Sunday afternoon. Sunday night, Doug took his usual turn round the back before bed, dog-less by the empty pond, down the path and out to the car; with a shotgun wrapped in a travel rug. He locked the gun in the boot, then went to bed. Had he lain awake at the enormity of it? Or had he slept at last, knowing it was nearly over? In the morning he drove out to Bedgebury Forest. Don saw him go, a careful driver in a brand-new car. He parked in a clearing under the trees. He took the shotgun from the boot and walked away from the car. He sat with his back against a tree, pointed the gun at his face and kicked the trigger, like his old Bantam. He didn't die. Instead, he staggered back to the car. Why, after going to the edge? The goodbye to his family, the new motor; is it why he learned to drive? Did the memories start reeling backwards as he bled? When Delmonden flashed up, did he wonder if it wasn't too late to go back? This time he knew it was bad, dear oh dear oh dear bad. All the kennel dogs a mile off made such a din, such a to-do at the shot. Now there was the shotgun to hide, the car keys to find, the slippery seat and poor Edna's steering wheel smeared in blood. Now he would have to *live* with what he had just done. He might clear it up, but they would have to know, for his own good, so they could send him to Farm Villa. He was driving a car, weeping blood, the sun setting in both eyes. How many sunsets had he fished, when the rivers ran clear, and he felt lucky to be alive? Here were the dogs, barking and howling as he pulled up outside the kennels and banged on the door for help. It was where all his Spaniels had come from. They were howling for his dripping blood, throwing themselves against the wire, like his trout. It's as far as I could go with him. It had all gone so badly across our fence. Then him dying like that in the ambulance. Fishing can never prevent that.

If ever a man needed a sign, this was surely it. There could be no retreating. I wouldn't say he hadn't died in vain, because he had. But while I remembered him, I'd fish for him, in the wake he'd made, until his ripples died away. It was all I desired of life, to be standing by water again, in the stupor of June, with carp rods, and a bite indicator moving slowly up to the butt ring, as slow as time itself, line tightening through the film, dragging a duck feather in its wake as the carp on the other end wallops the surface and the past shatters into a million fragments of light. That was thirty years ago, and the ripples have never died away.

At such a moment, I hesitate to write the end of the story. It abuses all point to existence, only it would be an error to risk bringing the shadow running through this book to a close. It has its own point; writing is as much at peril as fishing. The coming and the going of them has been my story. But for the shadow, there would have been no story.

On a bright spring day in 1982, I found myself on a train to Tunbridge Wells Central. I was on leave from Africa, now a freelance stringer for the World Service. The old wooden carriages stopped at empty stations. The orchards were in blossom. It was ten-to-two by the station clock in Tunbridge Wells. The cremation was at three. I was dressed head to foot in black, if unconventionally, for the occasion: a nurse's raincoat, roll neck, Yankee pants from Flip, black socks and lace-up plimsolls. The plimsolls were torn and stank, so I set off up Five Ways looking for a new pair. I found them in a dark, old-fashioned footwear store in Camden Road, put them on and slipped the old pair into a brown paper bag, rammed those into my raincoat pocket, then set off for the crematorium, picking up memories along the way. A favourite tearoom, Hall's bargain book box, up from a penny to twenty pence, the brown tomes in the window replaced by brash, glossy covers. Up the hill past Broadwater Down, our old college, now a secretarial school, the wilted gardens where. . . but there was no time for this. It was a quarter-to-three, ten years on. I began to run. The hill flattened out and I saw a line of black cars in the distance, creeping through a gateway across an empty sheet of green, pulling up outside the Athenaeum. I was sweating now, running harder. Down the long tarmac slope, mourners filed into the chapel. A few white crosses like rags of paper flapped on the green hills far away. I stopped in time, before running into the hearse. Twenty yards away, they were taking her out, shouldering the coffin, Sarah's father at the front. The pallbearers hesitated at the chapel door. In the memory, I see myself ducking under the coffin and slipping into a seat at the back, but there's an understandable blur over some of this. The coffin was lowered on to a slab at the front, a fancy coal bunker lined with flowers. The organ hissed like a wind in a scrapyard. No one shed tears, faces uncracked. Everyone wore grey, stiff backs and best scent, a few veiled hats, some of the men in darkish suits. I do not recall a single word of the service. The final organ piece drowned out the hum of the conveyor belt and the doors closed. Sarah was a ball of flame. She was twenty-seven. She'd been crossing The Strand outside Charing Cross station when a dispatch rider on a motorbike flew into her. After five days in a coma, the life support was turned off.

We filed out into daylight, past the wall of wreaths towards the car park. Most of the mourners went straight to their cars. I waited till Sarah's family appeared. They hadn't known I was coming. We stood awhile, it was a nice day, Claire liked my outfit, Connie said I looked well. They mentioned Sarah matter of factly. *She'd heard you were in London; she might have got in touch if, you know. . .* A man I didn't recognise introduced himself as if he was owed the respect of grief and felt neglected. The husband I knew she had left a few years back, dressed in an ill-fitting cheap grey suit with flared trousers. The second-best man I'd let Sarah down for. They were all going back to Hawkhurst. Connie had baked sausage rolls. There would be bread and cheese and apple juice and tea. I was pleased to be asked to join them, and the order of transport was being discussed when a man being led away by the arm suddenly turned and shouted my name, which he'd just heard mentioned, when Connie said *Dexter can go with Claire. . .*

The man was ten yards away. He held his hand out. At first I thought he was drunk and had flu, the flushed face, the tears streaming from his bloodshot eyes, the wide brimmed hat, black jacket, red roll neck. His voice a harsh whisper in its grief. The others shuffled away quietly.

'Are you Dexter ?' he said.

I nodded.

'Please,' he said, his throat convulsed in sobs, 'please, please come and see me. Ask Claire for my number. I was with Sarah. . . when it happened. We were holding hands. She was snatched out of my hand.'

He held the hand out again, making the shape of Sarah's hand inside it.

'Your name was in all her books,' he said.

A woman in a beret led him away. The others had waited by their cars. Nothing was said and I never saw him again. At the time, you don't always do what you should. It seemed a strange, but beautiful thing to say, that my name is in all her books, when her name is in all of mine.

THANK YOU:

Buj Stapley for bringing Ockley Pool back to life.
John Dawes of Hawkhurst, keeper, and giver, of its past.

Little Toller Books

We publish old and new writing attuned to nature and the landscape, working with a wide range of the very best writers and artists. We pride ourselves in publishing affordable books of the highest quality, which are designed and printed in south-west England. If you have enjoyed this book, you will also like exploring our list of other titles.

Field Notes

DEER ISLAND *Neil Ansell*

ORISON FOR A CURLEW *Horatio Clare*

LOVE MADNESS FISHING *Dexter Petley*

WATER AND SKY *Neil Sentance*

Monographs

HERBACEOUS *Paul Evans*

ON SILBURY HILL *Adam Thorpe*

THE ASH TREE *Oliver Rackham*

MERMAIDS *Sophia Kingshill*

BLACK APPLES OF GOWER *Iain Sinclair*

BEYOND THE FELL WALL *Richard Skelton*

ALLOTMENTS *David Crouch*

HAVERGEY *John Burnside*

SNOW *Marcus Sedgwick*

Nature Classics Library

THROUGH THE WOODS *H.E. Bates*

MEN AND THE FIELDS *Adrian Bell*

THE MIRROR OF THE SEA *Joseph Conrad*

ISLAND YEARS, ISLAND FARM *Frank Fraser Darling*

THE MAKING OF THE ENGLISH LANDSCAPE *W.G. Hoskins*

A SHEPHERD'S LIFE *W.H. Hudson*

BROTHER TO THE OX *Fred Kitchen*

FOUR HEDGES *Clare Leighton*

DREAM ISLAND *R.M. Lockley*

THE UNOFFICIAL COUNTRYSIDE *Richard Mabey*

RING OF BRIGHT WATER *Gavin Maxwell*

EARTH MEMORIES *Llewelyn Powys*

IN PURSUIT OF SPRING *Edward Thomas*

THE NATURAL HISTORY OF SELBORNE *Gilbert White*

A postcard sent to Little Toller will ensure you are put on our mailing list and amongst the first to discover each new book as it appears in the series. You can also follow our latest news at littletoller.co.uk or visit our online magazine theclearingonline.org for new essays, short films and poetry.

LITTLE TOLLER BOOKS

Lower Dairy, Toller Fratrum, Dorset DT2 0EL

W. littletoller.co.uk **E.** books@littletoller.co.uk